**LUCY SUMMERS** runs her own successful landscape design partnership, the Open Garden Company, which has both national international clients. As an RHS-qualified horticulturalist she has staged show gardens at the Chelsea Flower Show and has been awarded much-coveted Gold and Silver medals for her garden designs. She also contributes regularly to gardening publications, gives lectures to gardening clubs and organisations, and co-hosted *Britain's Best Back Gardens* for ITV among other television work. She lives in Surrey. This is the fifth title in the Greenfingers Guides series.

66 Trying to find a gardening book that is relevant to your needs isn't as straight-forward as it seems. Whether you are new to gardening or a dab hand, sometimes plant descriptions, including care, maintenance and general gardening jargon, can seem overly complicated or, worse still, just too vague. Greenfingers Guides cut through all this, delivering honest, practical information on a wide variety of beautiful plants with easy-to-follow layouts, all designed to enable you to get the best from your garden. Happy gardening! 99

GREENFINGERS GUIDES
# FRAGRANT PLANTS

## LUCY SUMMERS

headline

First published in 2011
by HEADLINE PUBLISHING GROUP

I

Lucy Summers would be happy to hear from readers
with their comments on the book at the following
e-mail address: lucy@greenfingersguides.co.uk

The Greenfingers Guides series concept was originated
by Lucy Summers and Darley Anderson

A CIP catalogue record for this title is available from
the British Library

ISBN 978 0 7553 6120 5

Design by Isobel Gillan
Printed and bound in Italy by Canale & C.S.p.A.

Headline's policy is to use papers that are natural,
renewable and recyclable products and made from wood
grown in sustainable forests. The logging and
manufacturing processes are expected to conform to the
environmental regulations of the country of origin.

HEADLINE PUBLISHING GROUP
An Hachette UK Company
338 Euston Road
London NW1 3BH

www.headline.co.uk
www.hachette.co.uk
www.greenfingersguides.co.uk
www.theopengardencompany.co.uk

DEDICATION
To Elle – the loveliest flower in my garden

OTHER TITLES IN THE GREENFINGERS GUIDES SERIES:

Drought-Tolerant Plants
ISBN 978 0 7553 1759 2

Fruit and Vegetables
ISBN 978 0 7553 1761 5

Climbers and Wall Shrubs
ISBN 978 0 7553 1758 5

Border Flowers
ISBN 978 0 7553 1760 8

# Contents

# Introduction

My entire early childhood can be conjured up in an intoxicating bouquet of fascinating, gratifying and nose-wrinkling whiffs. Ours was possibly the only school in the UK where the smell of overcooked cabbage didn't pervade the corridors. Instead, we were enveloped in comforting, homely aromas of fragrant buttery pastry, rising yeast and warm, fresh milk, merging with the smell of beeswaxed oak tainted with bleach (from the laundry across the way), all curiously synthesised by the light floral draught of laburnum wafting in from across the garden. The sweet, fresh scent of daffodils; the caustic smack of rotting manure on the flowerbeds; the pungent whiff of the herb garden and the unmistakable cat pee smell of the topiary being clipped in summer still evoke enchanted memories.

The fruits and spoils of the kitchen garden, greenhouses and orchards, each with their unique olfactory signatures, offered a rich supplement to our school menu and we were encouraged to express an interest in growing them. It wasn't that we were precocious gardeners. In truth, Mr Setek, the school gardener, Knower-of-all-Growing-Things, did the growing; we kids were the expert foragers and gorgers. He was our leader and we were his eager troupe.

From January to April, we were on red alert for the summons to the cool, ancient dampness of the scullery, where we excitedly awaited the issue of a plastic beaker half full of sugar. This was our cue to race off to the rhubarb patch, where Mr Setek, a past master at rhubarb-forcing, distributed each eager child with a whopping great ruby wand of the stuff, which we dipped in the sugar, chewing and sucking greedily at its tart sweetness.

Oh yes, that man knew how to grow things. He knew just how to prune fruit-bearing trusses to ensure a bumper harvest; how and when to stool the raspberry canes, with their woody-sweet reek; he taught us to stroke gooseberries, testing them between finger and thumb for ripeness, or pluck crisp, bright green lettuces from their neat, earthy rows. We dug cool, soil-dusty potatoes, pulled vibrant orange carrots, bruised aromatic herbs and netted and tangled many a fruit bush. We dared each other to invade the inner sanctum of his cedar potting shed, where fascinating glass bottles of forbidden, murky-coloured, acrid liquids stood on cobwebby shelves, mingled with the tang of mud and resin.

He encouraged us to wander along the hedgerows in the mellow late summer, collecting plump, earthy-scented blackberries which we delivered in metal pails to the kitchen door, for cook to add to fragrant crumbles and pies. And once the day's exertions were done, we would collapse, sweaty and happy, our stomachs distended and eyes squinting into the warming sun, with the drone of the mower buzzing peaceably in the distance as Mr Setek striped the lawns, releasing the clean, fresh smell of newly mown grass on a perfect summer's afternoon. The sky was blue, with not a cloud in sight, and the very heavens smiled indulgently on our little piece of paradise.

OPPOSITE Fragrant bliss: a traditional summer garden patio with strawberries, herbs in pots and perfumed climbing plants

# Choosing fragrant plants

Imagine a garden without fragrance. It's unthinkable. Every minor or major milestone in life has its own sensory bookmark of aroma that can summon up past happiness or sorrow with one sudden draught. Which of us has not been hopelessly seduced by the exotic scent of jasmine on a warm summer's evening or beguiled by the spicy draught of a flowering rose?

Shape, foliage and flower are all important when choosing garden plants but, stepping away from a very fragrant *Viburnum burkwoodii* in my garden in spring, I am reminded that its heavenly perfume was a deciding factor when I chose it. Why is its scent so powerful? There is an opulent richness to the perfume at a time of year when fragrances tend to be light and fleeting. Perhaps it reminds me of warmer days ahead. It certainly makes me happy.

Writing a book about fragrant plants is like being invited to a sumptuous feast and then denied the pleasure of savouring each mouthwatering morsel. And no two gardeners will agree on the pleasantness of smells, particularly when the aromatic plants are concerned (what one finds astringent, another might find soothingly antiseptic). The scent of some plants, such as daffodils, lupins and scabious, drifts lightly on the air, while jasmine, drimys and roses seem to saturate the air around them, drenching it with perfume. Scratch 'n' sniff is needed here, but instead we will have to rely on our imaginations and sense memory.

Many herbaceous perennials, such as richly potent pinks and sweetly distinctive phlox, have scents that are instantly recognisable. They tempt us towards them, creating delightful odorous intervals in summer flowerbeds and borders. Bulbs make fragrant pockets in the garden throughout the year, from snowdrops in winter to shivering daffodils planted through rough grass in spring or summer-flowering lilies and crinums in pots and borders. They are fabulous for adding hidden layers and textures to existing planting. You may need to stoop to inhale a deep breath of their sweetness, but this only reminds us not to overlook them just because they're small.

Trees and shrubs often have characteristic smells: think of the lily of the valley scent of mahonia and the bubble-gum sweetness of cistus, or the vanilla confection of great waxy bowls of magnolia. You can't really go wrong with a scented shrub. Whether deciduous or evergreen, most bring the joyful union of interesting foliage and fragrance to a garden. Some even have ornamental berries in autumn, so they score highly on year-round features. And they tend to need very little maintenance.

The many aromatic plants, including popular favourites like lavender, rosemary, sage and mint, carry their scent in oils in their foliage. In some, such as camphorus santolina and the spicy curry plant, the leaves need to be crushed or bruised to release the aroma, while others are activated by hot sun. Whether musky, minty, citrus or spicy, these scents are usually subtler than a sweet, fragrant flower perfume.

Roses are renowned for their incredibly diverse range of scents, but any plant that has been specifically bred for certain characteristics (such as better disease resistance or longer flowering) often has very little or no scent; as a general rule of thumb, the old-fashioned roses are likely to have a higher 'whiff' factor than their modern hybrid counterparts. However,

if you simply have to have a particularly lovely, old-fashioned, heavily scented rose, even though it may be vulnerable to a number of deeply inconvenient rose maladies, then you choose perfume over hardship – and what brave soul would argue that the trade-off is not worthwhile?

Let this book guide you to growing plants with fragrances that will elevate your garden from the ordinary to the simply magical.

RIGHT *Clematis armandii* is a magnet for nectar-collecting insects

## Using this book

Each plant listed is categorised according to its flowering season and eventual height, with useful, practical cultivation advice that will encourage you to grow with ever greater enjoyment, creativity and confidence. More detailed information, covering all the different elements mentioned in the profiles, and including help with planting and propagation, can be found after the plant profiles. There are lists of plants for specific purposes at the back of the book.

Throughout the book, plants are arranged seasonally, but in practice the corresponding months will vary according to local weather patterns, regional differences and the effects of climate change. Additionally, the flowering times of many plants span more than one season. The seasons given are based in this country, and should be thought of as a flexible guide.

| | | | |
|---|---|---|---|
| Early spring | March | Early autumn | September |
| Mid-spring | April | Mid-autumn | October |
| Late spring | May | Late autumn | November |
| Early summer | June | Early winter | December |
| Mid-summer | July | Mid-winter | January |
| Late summer | August | Late winter | February |

Latin names have been given for all the plants in this book because these are the names that are universally used when describing plants; the Latin name should be instantly recognised by the garden centre, and with any luck you will be sold the right plant. Common names have also been given, but these vary from country to country, and even within a country, and a plant may not always be recognised by its common name.

Skill level is indicated by one of three ratings:
**EASY, MEDIUM** or **TRICKY**

Many of the plants chosen for this book have been given the Award of Garden Merit (AGM) by the Royal Horticultural Society (RHS). This is a really useful pointer in helping you decide which plants to buy. The AGM is intended to be of practical value to the ordinary gardener, and plants that merit the award are the cream of the crop. The RHS is continually assessing new plant cultivars and you can be sure that any plant with an AGM will have excellent decorative features and be:

- easily available to the buying public
- easy to grow and care for
- not particularly susceptible to pests or disease
- robust and healthy

# SPRING

We've made it through the dark, bleak, frostbitten early winter mornings and charcoal black afternoons and are anxiously scanning the skies for some hopeful glimmer of warmer, sunnier days on the way. A tiny green shoot wavering uncertainly above cold earth, a young leaf bud timidly unfurling or the precocious flowering of dainty winter snowdrops remind us once again that the world turns and brighter days beckon. Fragrant spring plants aren't numerous – after all, it's still a bit early for the bees and insects which pollinate them – but some brave individuals are happy to flower and fragrance the garden without flinching at the inhospitable weather.

## *Anemone sylvestris*
### Snowdrop anemone

⬆ 30–50cm/12–20in ↔ 30–50cm/12–20in    **EASY**

This suckering, herbaceous perennial from northern Europe is a tough little contender with appealing, deeply divided bright green foliage in neat carpeting mounds. Each short, straight, wiry green-brown stem is topped with a pure white snowdrop-like flower bud, opening to simple, slightly nodding, five-petalled, shallow saucer-shaped, sweetly scented white flowers (up to 8cm/3in across) with golden stamens. White woolly seed heads follow the flowers. *A.s.* 'Flore Pleno' is a lovely white double-flowered variety.

**BEST USES** Ideal for pots and informal or formal garden borders; does well in coastal gardens; leave undisturbed to naturalise in a woodland garden; good as cut flowers

**FLOWERS** April to May

**ASPECT** Any, in a sheltered or exposed position; full sun to partial shade

**SOIL** Any fertile, moist, well-drained soil

**HARDINESS** Fully hardy at temperatures down to -15°C/5°F; needs no winter protection

**DROUGHT TOLERANCE** Poor

**PROBLEMS** Caterpillars, slugs and snails; powdery mildew

**CARE** Deadhead to encourage further flowering; remove dead and damaged leaves; cut back to just above ground level in late winter or spring

**PROPAGATION** Best by division in early spring; sow ripe seed immediately in a cold frame in autumn (but germination can be patchy and slow)

## *Arabis alpina* subsp. *caucasica* 'Flore Pleno' Wall rock cress

⬆ 15cm/6in ⬌ Indefinite          **EASY**

Would you believe this dainty perennial belongs to the brassica family? Look closely and you will see that the leaves have a passing 'cabbagey' character. This quick-growing evergreen plant is found widely in mountainous areas in southern Europe. The slim, toothed rosettes of grey-green leaves form a pleasing dense carpet, and slender, loose stems bear clusters of small, sweetly fragrant, star-shaped double white flowers in mid to late spring.

**BEST USES** Perfect in alpine troughs, cascading over drystone walls, or at the front of a raised bed

**FLOWERS** May

**ASPECT** South, west or east facing, in a sheltered or exposed position; full sun

**SOIL** Any poor, well-drained soil

**HARDINESS** Fully hardy at temperatures down to -15°C/5°F; needs no winter protection

**DROUGHT TOLERANCE** Good, once established

**PROBLEMS** Aphids; downy mildew and clubroot

**CARE** Cut back flower stems lightly after flowering

**PROPAGATION** Softwood cuttings in summer; sow seed in a cold frame in autumn

**GREENFINGER TIP** *For all its dainty good looks, this is a tough plant and it can be invasive: pull up any unwanted spread as it occurs*

## *Convallaria majalis* Lily of the valley

⬆ 23cm/9in ⬌ 30cm/12in          **EASY**

Come, now – which of you hasn't heard of lily of the valley? From temperate regions across the globe, this slow-creeping, rhizomatous perennial seems to strike a fond note with gardeners everywhere. Its deep green, stemless, veined, broadly elliptical leaves have crisp modern lines, and the short, sturdy, smooth green stems are hung with tiny, nodding, bell-shaped pure white waxen flowers with a distinctive lily fragrance. If you want to hunt down the Rolls-Royce of convallarias, look out for the coveted cream-striped leaves of *C.m.* 'Albostriata'.

**BEST USES** Any gloomy city garden benefits from the fresh green foliage, and the snow white flowers add a dash of brightness to a dull corner or woodland garden; does well in a bog or wildflower garden

**FLOWERS** May to June

**ASPECT** Any, in a sheltered position; partial to full shade

**SOIL** Any fertile, moist, humus-rich soil

**HARDINESS** Fully hardy at temperatures down to -15°C/5°F; needs no winter protection

**DROUGHT TOLERANCE** Poor

**PROBLEMS** *Botrytis* (grey mould)

**CARE** Low maintenance; mulch with leafmould or organic matter annually in early spring

**PROPAGATION** Dig up established clumps in autumn, separate rhizomes and replant with leafmould

## *Daphne cneorum* 'Eximia' ♀
Garland flower

⬆ 15cm/6in ⬌ 2m/6ft                    **EASY**

This almost prostrate evergreen shrub from central and southern Europe is a little more energetic in its growth habit than some of the very slow-growing species, so is marvellous for the smaller garden. It has small, oval, dark green leaves that densely clothe its stems, and the luxuriant clusters of tightly rounded deep pink flower buds open to simple, shallow, star-shaped rose pink flowers, which are deeply fragrant, and are often followed by beige berries.

**BEST USES** Ideal for a container or pot; perfect for the cottage garden or lightly shaded patio

**FLOWERS** May

**ASPECT** South, west or east facing, in a sheltered position with protection from cold winds; full sun to partial shade

**SOIL** Any fertile, moist, humus-rich, well-drained soil

**HARDINESS** Fully hardy at temperatures down to -15°C/5°F; needs no winter protection

**DROUGHT TOLERANCE** Poor

**PROBLEMS** Aphids; *Botrytis* (grey mould)

**CARE** Prune minimally; remove dead, damaged or diseased wood in late winter

**PROPAGATION** Layering in spring; semi-ripe cuttings in mid to late summer

## *Dianthus* 'Mrs Sinkins'
Pink

⬆ 45cm/18in ⬌ 20cm/8in                **EASY**

Pinks are traditional cottage garden favourites, native to Europe and Asia. Clump-forming evergreen perennials, they have a neat habit and heavenly fragrance, assuring them a place in garden borders for years to come. This old-fashioned pink undoubtedly has the most potent fragrance of all, with small, narrow, grey-green leaves and slender stems, knobbled at intervals, bearing very pretty, clove-scented, double white, fringed flowers. *D.* 'Bailey's Celebration' has coconut-ice colouring; *D.* 'Monica Wyatt' ♀ has lavender-pink flowers and *D.* 'Widecombe Fair' ♀ has pastel, creamy pink flowers.

**BEST USES** Ideal for edging paths or borders; happy in containers; does well in gravel gardens as fragrant ground cover; excellent cut flowers

**FLOWERS** May to June

**ASPECT** South, west or east facing, in a sheltered or exposed position; full sun

**SOIL** Any fertile, moist, well-drained soil

**HARDINESS** Fully hardy at temperatures down to -15°C/5°F; needs no winter protection

**DROUGHT TOLERANCE** Good, once established

**PROBLEMS** Aphids, slugs and snails; rust

**CARE** Deadhead regularly to encourage further flowering; remove dead flower stems in autumn

**PROPAGATION** Softwood cuttings (known as 'slips' or 'pipings') from non-flowering shoots in summer

## *Erysimum* 'Moonlight'
### Wallflower

⬆ 25cm/10in ⬌ 45cm/18in **EASY**

This carpeting short-lived Iberian evergreen
perennial is a pleasing cottage garden favourite.
It has a spreading habit, with small, narrow,
lance-shaped dark green leaves, and short,
branching stems topped with clusters of sweetly
scented, simple-petalled flowers (1cm/½in across)
which are luminous primrose yellow and a real
lure for bees and pollinating insects. It has a long
flowering period and is pretty unfussy, putting up
with poor soils as easily as more fertile ones,
though full sun is imperative.

**BEST USES** Eternally popular as edging for the
front of borders; perfect for a coastal, wildflower or
wildlife garden; thrives in pots and containers

**FLOWERS** March to June

**ASPECT** South or west facing, in a sheltered position;
full sun

**SOIL** Any poor to fertile, well-drained soil

**HARDINESS** Fully hardy at temperatures down to
-15°C/5°F; needs no winter protection

**DROUGHT TOLERANCE** Good, once established

**PROBLEMS** Cabbage root fly, flea beetles, slugs and
snails; clubroot, downy mildew and white blister

**CARE** Trim lightly after flowering to keep plant tidy

**PROPAGATION** Sow seed in pots in a cold frame in
spring and keep seedlings frost free; softwood cuttings
in late spring to summer

## *Galium odoratum*
### Woodruff

⬆ 45cm/18in ⬌ Indefinite **EASY**

Woodruff is a much-maligned rhizomatous
perennial from across Europe, noted for its
tendency to become invasive. However, when
kept within bounds, it is a charming plant with
appealing, bright green, deeply cut, dense
carpeting foliage that ages to deep green and
gives off the aroma of freshly cut hay when
bruised. From late spring right through to mid-
summer it sends up short, grooved stems topped
with clusters of small, star-shaped, honey-scented
snow white flowers, which are irresistible to bees.

**BEST USES** Excellent as ground cover in woodland
or shady gardens; ideal for covering awkward slopes
and banks; a great plant for wildlife gardens

**FLOWERS** May to July

**ASPECT** North or east facing, in a sheltered position;
full sun to partial shade

**SOIL** Any humus-rich, fertile, well-drained soil

**HARDINESS** Fully hardy at temperatures down to
-15°C/5°F; needs no winter protection

**DROUGHT TOLERANCE** Good, once established

**PROBLEMS** None

**CARE** Trim lightly in early to mid-spring; cut back older
straggly plants to ground level in spring

**PROPAGATION** Division in spring or autumn; sow ripe
seed immediately in a cold frame

## *Gladiolus tristis*
### Gladioli

⬆ 90cm/3ft ⬌ 5cm/2in      **MEDIUM**

This half-hardy South African cormous perennial does not tolerate extreme cold, but a little winter nursing should see it through our ever milder winters. It has long, straight, smooth, very narrow, reed-like mid-green leaves and wiry stems with pale green flat flower buds at intervals. These open to a trio of flared, trumpet-like flowers (up to 8cm/3in long) that are pale creamy yellow flushed green, with an almond scent that is most noticeable as evening falls. The petals are often stippled bronze, with a single deeper yellow stripe down the centre.

> **BEST USES** Adds height, elegance and heady perfume to the spring border when taller flowering plants are a bit of a rarity

**FLOWERS** April

**ASPECT** South or west facing, in a sheltered position; full sun

**SOIL** Any fertile, well-drained soil

**HARDINESS** Half hardy at temperatures down to 0°C/32°F; needs winter and frost protection

**DROUGHT TOLERANCE** Poor

**PROBLEMS** Aphids, slugs and snails; *Botrytis* (grey mould) and gladiolus corm rot

**CARE** Plant corms 15cm/6in deep in spring; dig up plants when leaves start to brown and remove to a frost-free greenhouse or porch through the winter; replant after all frost risk has passed

**PROPAGATION** Sow seed at 15°C/59°F in spring

## *Hemerocallis dumortieri*
### Day lily

⬆ 50cm/20in ⬌ 45cm/18in      **EASY**

Day lilies are evergreen or semi-evergreen clump-forming herbaceous perennials from Asia, and I am mad about them – for their flower shape, foliage, colours, fragrance and fascinating names. This cultivar has stiff, upright, narrow strap-like bright green foliage with tall, elegant, arching stems holding sweetly fragrant, yellow-gold flared trumpets (up to 8cm/3in long) with streaked brown markings on the petals. It flowers almost six weeks earlier than most day lilies (as early as mid-April in a warm year). Each bloom lasts only a day, but another takes its place the next morning.

> **BEST USES** Fabulous with ornamental grasses in a formal border or cottage garden; good in containers; rabbit proof

**FLOWERS** May to June

**ASPECT** South, west or east facing, in a sheltered or exposed position; full sun

**SOIL** Any fertile, moist, well-drained soil

**HARDINESS** Fully hardy at temperatures down to -15°C/5°F; needs no winter protection

**DROUGHT TOLERANCE** Good, once established

**PROBLEMS** None

**CARE** Mulch annually in spring; deadhead daily; cut stems to the ground when flowering is over

**PROPAGATION** Division in spring or autumn

## Hermodactylus tuberosus
### Snake's head iris

⬆ 40cm/16in ⬌ 5cm/2in     **EASY**

There is only one species of this slightly unusual tuberous perennial from south-east Europe (and you may need to go to a specialist nursery to find it) but it's a pretty thing, offering both colour and fragrance in spring. It has linear, narrow, grassy leaves (up to 45cm/18in long) and smooth, straight, squarish stems bearing iris-like flowers (about 5cm/2in long). The clove-scented flowers have curiously coloured drooping petals of greenish creamy yellow with brown-maroon markings at the tips. It will put up with any soil that is well drained, but sun is essential.

**BEST USES** Naturalise in rough, grassy areas; ideal at the front of informal borders; perfect for containers and pots on a sunny city patio

**FLOWERS** March to May

**ASPECT** South, west or east facing, in a sheltered position with protection from cold winds; full sun

**SOIL** Any fertile, humus-rich, well-drained soil, including chalk

**HARDINESS** Fully hardy at temperatures down to -15°C/5°F; needs no winter protection

**DROUGHT TOLERANCE** Good, once established

**PROBLEMS** Can be short-lived

**CARE** Cut back to maintain desired size and spread in spring or late summer

**PROPAGATION** Division after flowering

**GREENFINGER TIP** *This can take a year or so to settle down and start flowering freely, and will spread slowly*

## Hesperis matronalis var. albiflora
### Sweet rocket

⬆ 90cm/3ft ⬌ 45cm/18in     **EASY**

This tall, clump-forming perennial, from Asia across to central Europe, is often grown as a biennial as it is short-lived. Clothed in narrow, bristly, dark green leaves, it has strong, erect, tall branching stems topped with domed clusters of simple, clove-scented, four-petalled pure white flowers from late spring. A full complement of pollen-collecting visitors is always in attendance. *H. matronalis* is similar, with pale mauve flowers.

**BEST USES** Ideal in a wildlife garden; does well in cottage garden borders or a woodland garden

**FLOWERS** May to June

**ASPECT** South, west or east facing, in a sheltered or exposed position; full sun to partial shade

**SOIL** Any fertile, moist, well-drained soil

**HARDINESS** Fully hardy at temperatures down to -15°C/5°F; needs no winter protection

**DROUGHT TOLERANCE** Good, once established

**PROBLEMS** Caterpillars, slugs and snails; powdery mildew

**CARE** Remove spent flowering stems; replace plants every three years or so

**PROPAGATION** Self-seeds easily; basal cuttings in spring

**GREENFINGER TIP** *This white variety comes true from seed if grown without any mauve varieties; pull up unwanted colour variations*

## Hyacinthus orientalis 'City of Haarlem' ⚜ Hyacinth

⬆ 30cm/12in ⬌ 8cm/3in                    EASY

These hardy bulbous perennials originate from Asia and come in a wide colour range, from china blue through purple, fuchsia and pale pink to yellows and whites. They have erect, strap-like mid-green leaves and stout, upright, smooth green flower stems densely packed with small, single, tubular, scented flowers clustered tightly together to form pillared flower heads. They can be grown outside in the garden or potted up to enjoy indoors. This enchanting variety has sweetly fragrant clear primrose yellow flowers. *H.o.* 'Blue Jacket' ⚜ has dark blue flowers, *H.o.* 'Delft Blue' ⚜ is pastel blue and *H.o.* 'Woodstock' has rich cerise blooms.

> **BEST USES** Perfect for cottage gardens and spring or woodland borders; thrives in pots

**FLOWERS** March to April (January indoors)
**ASPECT** Any, in a sheltered position; full sun to partial shade
**SOIL** Any fertile, moist, well-drained soil; pot-grown plants dislike winter wet
**HARDINESS** Fully hardy at temperatures down to -15°C/5°F; needs no winter protection
**DROUGHT TOLERANCE** Poor
**PROBLEMS** Narcissus bulb fly and narcissus eelworms
**CARE** Plant outdoor bulbs 10cm/4in deep and 8–15cm/3–6in apart, from late summer to autumn (for indoor bulbs, see page 101)
**PROPAGATION** Buy fresh bulbs annually

## Loropetalum chinense f. rubrum 'Fire Dance' Chinese witch hazel

⬆ 90cm/3ft ⬌ 90cm/3ft                    EASY

At a quick glance you would never guess that this rounded evergreen shrub of Asian origin belongs to the witch hazel family (commonly noted for their yellow flowers). It has oval leaves that are deep claret-coloured when young, deepening to burgundy in late summer through to autumn: this shrub is worth growing for the leaves alone. Add in the clusters of small, spidery, very sweetly fragrant pink flowers that appear in early spring (or even late winter) and you have an out-and-out winner of a shrub that looks good all year. It is destined to become one of the most prized shrubs in your garden.

> **BEST USES** Excellent grown against a warm wall or trained as a wall shrub in a sunny courtyard garden or patio; ideal container plant

**FLOWERS** March
**ASPECT** Any, in a sheltered position; full sun to partial shade
**SOIL** Any fertile, humus-rich, moist, well-drained, slightly acid soil
**HARDINESS** Frost hardy at temperatures down to -5°C/23°F; needs winter protection
**DROUGHT TOLERANCE** Poor
**PROBLEMS** None
**CARE** Trim lightly after flowering
**PROPAGATION** Sow ripe seed immediately in a cold frame; semi-ripe cuttings in a heated propagator in summer

## Maianthemum racemosum

(formerly *Smilacina racemosa*) False spikenard

⬆ 90cm/3ft ⬌ 60cm/24in                    EASY

Native to both North America and Mexico, this rhizomatous perennial woodlander can be slow to settle down, but makes a sizeable clump within three years. The elliptical pointed mid-green leaves, paired along smooth green arching stems, are heavily vein-etched. Tall flower stems support generous numbers of foamy flower spikes, with lightly scented creamy white flowers, around the middle of spring. The mottled brown green berries that follow the flowers ripen to deep red and are said to be rich in vitamins, purportedly tasting of bitter molasses. Here's an interesting snippet of information: the native Indians of North America used this plant medicinally as a form of contraception and to treat body pains and cancer.

> **BEST USES** Very effective as ground cover in a shady or woodland garden; ideal for bringing a splash of light to shadowy city gardens

**FLOWERS** April to June

**ASPECT** North, east or west facing, in a sheltered position with protection from cold winds; partial to full shade

**SOIL** Any fertile, humus-rich, moist, well-drained, acid soil

**HARDINESS** Fully hardy at temperatures down to -15°C/5°F; needs no winter protection

**DROUGHT TOLERANCE** Poor

**PROBLEMS** Slugs and snails

**CARE** Cut back to ground level in late winter

**PROPAGATION** Division in spring

## Narcissus 'Tripartite'

Daffodil

⬆ 45cm/18in ⬌ 15cm/6in                    EASY

Everyone associates daffodils with spring. These upright bulbous perennials from Europe to North Africa have erect, narrow, smooth, strappy green leaves and smooth, leafless stems. There are numerous species (not all fragrant), with large or small flower trumpets, solitary or multiple flowers, some with nodding flowers or reflexed petals, in shades of gold, orange, white, cream and pinky hues. This sweetly scented variety has small, golden multi-flower heads, one per stem. It is so free flowering that it makes me sublimely happy.

> **BEST USES** Excellent in spring borders or mixed shrub borders; very easy in containers or pots; naturalises beautifully in wild grassy areas

**FLOWERS** May

**ASPECT** Any, in a sheltered or exposed position; full sun to partial shade

**SOIL** Any fertile, moist, well-drained soil

**HARDINESS** Fully hardy at temperatures down to -15°C/5°F; needs no winter protection

**DROUGHT TOLERANCE** Poor

**PROBLEMS** Narcissus bulb fly and narcissus eelworms; narcissus basal rot

**CARE** Plant bulbs to twice their depth in autumn; deadhead flowers, but leave foliage to die back naturally

**PROPAGATION** Division of large clumps after flowering, when leaves are browning; offsets in early autumn

## *Oxalis enneaphylla*

⬆ 10cm/4in ⬌ 15cm/6in     **EASY**

This diminutive mat-forming tuberous perennial is native to South America and the Falkland Islands. It has very attractive, pale grey-green, spoon-like leaves (about 2cm/¾in long), arranged like circular pleated fans and forming soft mounds. Short, smooth, pinkish stems carry single, cupped, white and pink almond-scented flowers. These open in bright sunlight and remain steadfastly shut in overcast conditions and at night. *O.e.* 'Sheffield Swan' has ivory white flowers; *O.e.* 'Rosea' has pale pink flowers.

**BEST USES** A dear little plant for cottage gardens, at the front of borders and edging paths and flowerbeds; ideal for rock gardens and containers

**FLOWERS** May to June

**ASPECT** Any, in a sheltered position; full sun to partial shade

**SOIL** Any fertile, moist, well-drained soil

**HARDINESS** Fully hardy at temperatures down to -15°C/5°F; needs no winter protection

**DROUGHT TOLERANCE** Poor

**PROBLEMS** Slugs and snails; rust

**CARE** Can become invasive, so dig up any unwanted spread

**PROPAGATION** Division in spring

## *Polygonatum odoratum*
### Solomon's seal

⬆ 85cm/34in ⬌ 50cm/20in     **EASY**

Among my top ten perennials, Solomon's seal is a rhizomatous perennial that spreads by creeping and is found from Japan to Russia and Europe. Its smooth, lightly veined, fresh green leaves (up to 15cm/6in long) provide perfect, elegant arches from which dangle pairs of sweetly scented, tubular white flowers, flushed apple green at the tips, in late spring. These are followed by small, inedible, round black berries, which are an appealing feature. *P.o.* 'Flore Pleno' is slightly taller (55cm/22in) and has creamy double flowers. All parts of the plant are toxic.

**BEST USES** Ideal in a shady or woodland garden among ferns, foxgloves and hardy geraniums; its clean lines make it perfect for modern city gardens; deer and rabbit proof

**FLOWERS** May

**ASPECT** Any, in a sheltered position; partial to full shade

**SOIL** Any fertile, moist, well-drained soil; add organic matter or leafmould before planting

**HARDINESS** Fully hardy at temperatures down to -15°C/5°F; needs no winter protection

**DROUGHT TOLERANCE** Poor

**PROBLEMS** Sawfly larvae, slugs and snails

**CARE** Mulch in spring

**PROPAGATION** Division as new growth starts in spring (separate creeping runners carefully as they can be brittle and break easily)

## *Primula vulgaris* 🏅
### Wild primrose

⬆ 20cm/8in ⬌ 35cm/14in       EASY

Its simple elegance makes this semi-evergreen native perennial instantly recognisable. The coarse, spoon-shaped, fresh green leaves, with etched veining, are arranged in appealing rosettes, and short, softly bristled stems arise from these low leafy mounds, each topped with sweetly fragrant, single, pale yellow flowers (up to 4cm/1½in across) with darker yellow eyes. *P.v.* 'Alba Plena' is a lovely double-flowered white variety.

**BEST USES** Naturalises well in wild grassy areas or along banks; ideal for the small cottage garden, wildflower or woodland garden; delightful in pots or containers in north-facing gardens

**FLOWERS** March to May
**ASPECT** Any, in a sheltered position; partial to full shade
**SOIL** Any fertile, humus-rich, moist, well-drained soil
**HARDINESS** Fully hardy at temperatures down to -15°C/5°F; needs no winter protection
**DROUGHT TOLERANCE** Poor
**PROBLEMS** *Botrytis* (grey mould) and leaf spot
**CARE** Deadhead to prevent self-seeding
**PROPAGATION** Sow ripe seed immediately; division every two years in late spring or autumn, to maintain flowering

## *Skimmia japonica* 'Fragrans' 🏅

⬆ 90cm/3ft ⬌ 90cm/3ft       EASY

This evergreen, mounded shrub from Asia is neatly attired with elliptical, glossy deep green, slightly aromatic leaves on short, sturdy, contrasting reddish brown stems. These bear generous clusters of tiny, white, lily of the valley-scented bell-shaped flowers that open from tight pink buds. Many skimmia (though not all) need both male and female plants to produce fruit, so you will need plants of both sexes if you want the red berry display on the female plants. This variety is male, so has no berries.

**BEST USES** Ideal for north-facing or shady gardens; does well in woodland; unbeatable as ground cover

**FLOWERS** April to May
**ASPECT** Any, in a sheltered or exposed position; partial to full shade
**SOIL** Any fertile, well-drained soil
**HARDINESS** Fully hardy at temperatures down to -15°C/5°F; needs no winter protection
**DROUGHT TOLERANCE** Good, once established
**PROBLEMS** Scale insects
**CARE** Trim lightly after flowering, to maintain size and shape
**PROPAGATION** Semi-ripe cuttings in a heated propagator in late summer

**GREENFINGER TIP** *Would you believe that female plants are usually more fragrant than the males? Rather like us then ...*

## Trillium luteum
### Wake robin

⬆ 40cm/16in ⬌ 30cm/12in          **EASY**

Trilliums are clump-forming rhizomatous woodlanders, native to the UK. This yellow species from the USA is among the easiest to grow and has oval, dark green leaves (about 15cm/6in long) with marbled lighter splashes of green, spaced equally at the top of the stem. The stemless, lemony-scented mid-yellow flowers form upright, open, gappy goblets in the centre of the leaves. The plant dies back in autumn, reappearing the following year. This self-seeds freely but slowly, so leave seedlings to colonise.

**BEST USES** Ideal in woodland or wildlife gardens and in shady city borders; pretty by ponds and streams, at the water's edge

**FLOWERS** March to April

**ASPECT** North, east or west facing, in a sheltered position; partial to full shade

**SOIL** Any fertile, moist, well-drained soil; dislikes heavy clay soils

**HARDINESS** Fully hardy at temperatures down to -15°C/5°F; needs no winter protection

**DROUGHT TOLERANCE** Poor

**PROBLEMS** Slugs and snails

**CARE** None

**PROPAGATION** Self-seeds easily; sow ripe seed immediately in pots in a shaded cold frame; division of rhizomes in spring after flowering

**GREENFINGER TIP** *Planting dried rhizomes can be unreliable, so grow from potted plants if possible*

## Vitaliana primuliflora
### Golden primrose

⬆ 2.5cm/1in ⬌ 25cm/10in          **EASY**

Just looking at this neat little beauty is probably enough to tell you it comes from European alpine regions: it's easy to imagine it fiercely hugging any rocky, gravelly, gritty nook or crevice for survival. It is a mat-forming evergreen perennial with rosettes of small, softly bristled sage green leaves that make appealing thick rugs of foliage, smothered from early spring with freshly scented stemless, tubular, buttercup yellow flowers.

**BEST USES** Perfect for the rock garden, and in well-drained gravel or Mediterranean gardens; ideal for an alpine trough or shallow container

**FLOWERS** March to May

**ASPECT** South, west or east facing, in a sheltered or exposed position; full sun

**SOIL** Any fertile, moist, well-drained gritty or stony soil; dislikes sitting in winter wet

**HARDINESS** Fully hardy at temperatures down to -15°C/5°F; needs no winter protection

**DROUGHT TOLERANCE** Poor

**PROBLEMS** None

**CARE** None

**PROPAGATION** Self-seeds freely; remove rooted stems and pot them up in spring

**GREENFINGER TIP** *If you have a mound of builders' rubble that needs hiding, this is the perfect plant to cover it*

## *Berberis julianae*
### Julian's barberry

⬆ 2m/6ft ⬌ 1.5m/5ft          **EASY**

I'm not altogether keen on berberis, and I loathe their injurious spiny branches, but am pleased to make an exception for this dense, upright, evergreen Chinese shrub, as it has much to offer in year-round interest. It has small, elliptical grey-green leaves that flush attractive claret in autumn. The pliable stems are spiny (like most of the breed), so wear gloves when pruning. It bears lightly honey-scented, golden yellow, clustered flowers at intervals along the stems. These are at their best in early summer, but usually flower earlier. Glorious damson-coloured berries follow the flowers in autumn. It's a strong grower, so give it space from the outset.

**BEST USES** Ideal as a hedge to deter unwanted visitors; good for seaside gardens and north-facing walls

**FLOWERS** May to June

**ASPECT** Any, in a sheltered or exposed position; full sun to partial shade

**SOIL** Any fertile, moist, well-drained soil

**HARDINESS** Fully hardy at temperatures down to -15°C/5°F; needs no winter protection

**DROUGHT TOLERANCE** Good, once established

**PROBLEMS** None

**CARE** Minimal pruning in early spring, to maintain size and shape

**PROPAGATION** Semi-ripe cuttings in late summer; layering in autumn

## *Choisya* x *dewitteana* 'Aztec Pearl'
### Mexican orange blossom

⬆ 2.5m/8ft ⬌ 2.5m/8ft          **EASY**

This enduringly popular group of versatile evergreen shrubs, originally from the USA and Mexico, is famed for their handsome foliage and scented blossoms. This variety is more restrained than some in its growth habit, making it suitable for smaller spaces. It is a compact, rounded, evergreen shrub, with narrow, slender, glossy dark green leaves, and is smothered in abundant clusters of sweetly fragrant, pinky white flowers with short golden stamens in late spring. It often produces a second, more modest, flush of flowers from late summer into autumn.

**BEST USES** Ideal for low maintenance gardens; good for clothing awkward banks and slopes; lovely in the mixed border

**FLOWERS** May; repeating August/September

**ASPECT** South, west or east facing, in a sheltered position; full sun

**SOIL** Any fertile, well-drained soil

**HARDINESS** Fully hardy at temperatures down to -15°C/5°F; needs no winter protection

**DROUGHT TOLERANCE** Excellent, once established

**PROBLEMS** Snails

**CARE** Prune lightly after flowering, to maintain size and shape

**PROPAGATION** Semi-ripe cuttings in summer

**GREENFINGER TIP** *This will tolerate light shade but flowering is significantly reduced*

## *Corylopsis sinensis*
## Cowslip bush

⬆ 4m/13ft ↔ 4m/13ft                    **EASY**

An upright deciduous shrub from China, this has an open, spreading habit with oval, dark green leaves with densely downy, blue-tinged undersides. These appear after the dangling, pale primrose yellow flowers, which are displayed on bare brown stems in mid-spring and are cowslip-scented. *C.s.* var. *sinensis* 'Spring Purple' has decorative lemon yellow flowers and purple-tinted leaves and stems; *C.s.* var. *calvescens* f. *veitchiana* ⚕ (4m/13ft × 2.5m/8ft) has soft yellow flowers and larger, rounder, pink-hued leaves.

> **BEST USES** Ideal for the larger spring garden, mixed shrub border or shady woodland area; effective for brightening gloomy banks or slopes

**FLOWERS** April

**ASPECT** North, east or west facing, in a sheltered or exposed position; partial shade

**SOIL** Any fertile, moist, well-drained acid soil

**HARDINESS** Fully hardy at temperatures down to -15°C/5°F; needs no winter protection

**DROUGHT TOLERANCE** Poor

**PROBLEMS** None

**CARE** Remove any dead, diseased or damaged material in late winter

**PROPAGATION** Greenwood cuttings in summer; layering in autumn

**GREENFINGER TIP** *Plant with a scented summer-flowering clematis to make up for this plant's brief and early (but elegant) flowering display*

## *Dipelta floribunda* ⚕
## Rosy dipelta

⬆ 4m/13ft ↔ 4m/13ft                    **EASY**

This native Asian deciduous shrub isn't planted widely but it is every bit as good as the more popular spring-flowering shrubs such as lilac, and looks good for much of the year. It makes an upright, graceful, branching shrub with a moderate growth rate and appealing oval, light apple green leaves (10cm/4in across) that yellow in autumn. In late spring its arching stems are heavily laden with sweetly fragrant, funnelled, white-tinted shell pink flowers (about 4cm/1½in long) with golden orange throats staining the insides of the petals. It has the added bonus of attractive, pale green peeling bark in winter. *D. yunnanensis* is similar in appearance but more compact at 3m/10ft tall.

> **BEST USES** Excellent in a woodland garden or at the back of a sunny border

**FLOWERS** May to June

**ASPECT** South or west facing, in a sheltered position with protection from cold winds; full sun to partial shade

**SOIL** Any fertile, well-drained soil

**HARDINESS** Fully hardy at temperatures down to -15°C/5°F; needs no winter protection

**DROUGHT TOLERANCE** Good, once established

**PROBLEMS** None

**CARE** Cut back a few of the old stems to ground level after flowering, to encourage new basal growth and prevent legginess

**PROPAGATION** Softwood cuttings in summer

## *Fothergilla major*
### American witch hazel

⬆ 2.5m/8ft ⬌ 2m/6ft          MEDIUM

Native to the southern USA, this is a slow-growing, rounded, multi-stemmed deciduous shrub. The oval, mid-green leaves (the young foliage has a blush of bronze) are held on upright stems and begin to unfurl just after the sweetly perfumed, bottlebrush-like white blossoms have opened. The flowers are held at the tips of the branches and are made up of a mass of white stamens, rather than proper petals. In autumn the leaves develop fiery orange, red and yellow tints.

**BEST USES** Ideal for fragrant spring borders or wildlife gardens; adds late-autumn colour to a mixed border, shadowy patio or woodland garden

**FLOWERS** May to June

**ASPECT** Any, in a sheltered position; full sun to partial shade (flowering and autumn colour are reduced in shade)

**SOIL** Any fertile, humus-rich, moist, well-drained acid soil

**HARDINESS** Fully hardy at temperatures down to -15°C/5°F; needs no winter protection

**DROUGHT TOLERANCE** Poor

**PROBLEMS** None

**CARE** Remove any dead, diseased or damaged material after flowering or in late winter; mulch annually in early spring

**PROPAGATION** Sow seed in a cold frame in autumn; softwood cuttings (spray cuttings lightly with water every day) in summer

## *Lindera benzoin*
### Spice bush

⬆ 3m/10ft ⬌ 3m/10ft          EASY

This bushy deciduous shrub from the USA and Canada is slightly unusual, but nurseries are increasingly stocking it for its year-round interest. It has a moderate growth rate, with upright branches bearing aromatic, almost lavender-scented, large, leathery, oval, deep green leaves (some 13cm/5in long) after the flowers; the leaves fade to rich yellow in autumn. Tiny greeny yellow scented flowers (some 3mm/⅛in long) appear in spring at the tips of the bare branches and stems, followed by rich red, camphor-scented berries; even the stems and bark are aromatic.

**BEST USES** Ideal in woodland or wildlife gardens; excellent planted by ponds and streams; useful in mixed spring borders or shrubberies; makes good informal hedging

**FLOWERS** April

**ASPECT** Any, in a sheltered or exposed position; full sun to partial shade

**SOIL** Any fertile, moist, well-drained soil; tolerates acid soil

**HARDINESS** Fully hardy at temperatures down to -15°C/5°F; needs no winter protection

**DROUGHT TOLERANCE** Poor

**PROBLEMS** None

**CARE** Remove dead, diseased or damaged wood in late winter

**PROPAGATION** Semi-ripe cuttings in early summer

## Magnolia 'Susan' ♀

⬆ 3m/10ft ↔ 4m/13ft                    **EASY**

This deciduous Japanese shrub is the pick of the spring-flowering magnolias for fragrance. It is fairly slow-growing, compact and bushy, with a rather stiff, upright stance. In mid-spring, the bare branches are studded with large, upright, narrow, deep pinky purple buds that open to reveal sweetly fragrant tulip-shaped flowers of rich pinky purple. Large, oval, mid-green leaves open once the flowers have bloomed.

**BEST USES** Gorgeous as an architectural specimen in a lawn or large spring border, underplanted with bulbs; ideal for a cottage border

**FLOWERS** April to May

**ASPECT** Any, in a sheltered position; full sun

**SOIL** Any fertile, humus-rich, moist, well-drained soil; at its best on slightly acid soil

**HARDINESS** Fully hardy at temperatures down to -15°C/5°F; needs no winter protection

**DROUGHT TOLERANCE** Poor

**PROBLEMS** Capsid bugs

**CARE** Remove any dead, diseased or damaged material after flowering; mulch annually in early spring

**PROPAGATION** Semi-ripe cuttings in late summer

## Osmanthus x burkwoodii ♀

⬆ 3m/10ft ↔ 3m/10ft                    **EASY**

This neat, rounded, evergreen shrub of garden origin has much to recommend it for all seasons. It is densely clothed with lance-shaped, polished, deep laurel green leaves that have slightly serrated edges. Generous clusters of creamy flower buds, held on pale red stems, open to tubular, creamy white flowers with lemon-coloured anthers, flowering from mid to late spring. These are very fragrant. *O. delavayi* ♀ (6m/20ft × 4m/13ft) might be a better choice for the larger garden. It has clusters of tubular creamy fragrant flowers in spring.

**BEST USES** Ideal in a formal border or shrubbery, to add some evergreen bones for year-round interest; excellent for hedging

**FLOWERS** April to May

**ASPECT** Any, in a sheltered position, with protection from cold winds; full sun to partial shade

**SOIL** Any fertile, well-drained soil

**HARDINESS** Fully hardy at temperatures down to -15°C/5°F; needs no winter protection

**DROUGHT TOLERANCE** Good, once established

**PROBLEMS** None

**CARE** Trim individual plants and hedges lightly after flowering, removing dead, diseased or damaged material as you go

**PROPAGATION** Semi-ripe cuttings in summer in a heated propagator; layering in autumn or spring

## *Philadelphus* 'Belle Etoile' ♛
Mock orange

⬆ 1.2m/4ft ⬌ 2.5m/8ft          **EASY**

This deciduous shrub is one of the most popular and free flowering of the mock oranges, which hail from across Eastern Europe, Asia and Central America. It has arching, narrow, oval, fresh apple green leaves in spring and makes an explosive scented fountain, cascading with simple, shallowly cupped, highly perfumed pure white flowers with sherbet lemon-coloured stamens (about 5cm/2in across). The larger, faster growing *P.* 'Virginal' (3m/10ft or more tall) has a more erect habit, with equally intoxicating double white flowers.

**BEST USES** Perfect in the spring border or cottage garden; delightful planted along fences as an informal hedge; does well in coastal gardens

**FLOWERS** May to June
**ASPECT** Any, in a sheltered or exposed position; full sun to partial shade
**SOIL** Any fertile, well-drained soil
**HARDINESS** Fully hardy at temperatures down to -15°C/5°F; needs no winter protection
**DROUGHT TOLERANCE** Poor
**PROBLEMS** Aphids; powdery mildew
**CARE** Prune lightly after flowering; cut back one in four of the older stems to ground level every three or four years, to keep flowering evenly distributed
**PROPAGATION** Softwood cuttings in summer; hardwood cuttings in autumn or winter

## *Pittosporum tenuifolium* ♛

⬆ 3m/10ft ⬌ 1.5m/5ft          **EASY**

This bushy New Zealander makes a large, fairly fast-growing, evergreen shrub (or small tree), but its growth slows down with age. A lovely formal shrub, it has handsome, lance-shaped, glossy dark green leaves with wavy edges, rather like non-prickly holly. From late spring into early summer, it produces clusters of tubular damson-coloured honey-scented flowers with pretty, pale rose scales at the base and vivid lemony centres. Chubby, segmented seed pods follow the flowers, splitting open to reveal shiny, bible black seeds.

**BEST USES** Ideal in a woodland garden; adds formal elegance to a sunny border or container; can be used for hedging; excellent for coastal gardens

**FLOWERS** May
**ASPECT** Any, in a sheltered position with protection from cold winds; full sun to partial shade
**SOIL** Any fertile, moist, well-drained soil
**HARDINESS** Frost hardy at temperatures down to -5°C/23°F; needs winter protection
**DROUGHT TOLERANCE** Good, once established
**PROBLEMS** Powdery mildew
**CARE** Trim individual plants and hedges lightly in late winter, removing dead, diseased or damaged material as you go
**PROPAGATION** Semi-ripe cuttings in summer

## *Prunus mume* 'Beni-chidori'
**Japanese apricot**

 3m/10ft ⟷ 3m/10ft                    **EASY**

Despite its common name, this small, spreading tree, originating in the forests of western China, does not produce apricots. Earlier flowering than many of the ornamental cherries, it bears its double, cup-shaped, rich pink, almond-fragranced blossoms (2.5cm/1in across), with creamy eyelash stamens, on dark, bare stems in early spring before the leaves unfurl. The appealing foliage is pale fresh green in spring, maturing to pinky red tints in autumn.

> **BEST USES** Makes a graceful focal point in a lawn or flowering meadow; ideal for large containers on a warm sunny patio

**FLOWERS** March

**ASPECT** South or west facing, in a sheltered position with protection from cold winds; full sun

**SOIL** Any fertile, moist, well-drained soil

**HARDINESS** Fully hardy at temperatures down to -15°C/5°F; needs no winter protection

**DROUGHT TOLERANCE** Poor

**PROBLEMS** Aphids and caterpillars; blossom wilt, canker, honey fungus, peach leaf curl and silver leaf

**CARE** Remove dead, diseased or damaged material in summer (not winter), to prevent silver leaf

**PROPAGATION** Greenwood cuttings in early summer

························································

**GREENFINGER TIP** *I have often seen this flowering in late February after a mild winter*

## *Rhododendron fortunei* 'Sir Charles Butler'

 2m/6ft ⟷ 2.5m/8ft                    **EASY**

This upright to spreading evergreen shrub was discovered in China by plant hunter Robert Fortune in 1843. It has long, oval, dull deep green, leathery leaves and produces an extravagance of sweetly fragrant, funnel-shaped blooms (up to 8cm/3in long) that are white, blushed palest pink, in heavy trusses in late spring. I am informed that many of the newer Japanese varieties can thrive on limier soils.

> **BEST USES** Ideal for sheltered woodland or a shady spot in a gloomy garden

**FLOWERS** May to June

**ASPECT** Any, in a sheltered position with protection from cold winds; partial shade

**SOIL** Any fertile, humus-rich, moist, well-drained acid soil

**HARDINESS** Fully hardy at temperatures down to -15°C/5°F; needs no winter protection

**DROUGHT TOLERANCE** Poor

**PROBLEMS** Aphids, caterpillars, leafhoppers, scale insects and vine weevil; bud blast, honey fungus, powdery mildew, rust and silver leaf

**CARE** Plant shallowly, as they are surface rooting; trim lightly after flowering, removing dead, diseased or damaged material as you go

**PROPAGATION** Semi-ripe cuttings in late summer; layering in autumn

# Rhododendron 'Mary Poppins'

⬆ 2.5m/8ft ⬌ 1.5m/5ft                    **EASY**

Rhododendrons come from Asia, Australia, North America and Europe, so there is a huge range, grown for their flower displays. Many are scented. This deciduous shrub (formerly known as an azalea) is upright and very bushy, with elliptical deep green leaves that are flushed with fiery tints in autumn. The exuberant, large, honey-scented, bonfire-coloured, flame orange-red, funnel-shaped flowers have slightly crimped edges and appear in large clusters at the end of the branches.

**BEST USES** Perfect for a dappled woodland garden; makes an excellent flowering hedge

**FLOWERS** May

**ASPECT** Any, in a sheltered or exposed position; partial shade

**SOIL** Any fertile, humus-rich, well-drained acid soil

**HARDINESS** Fully hardy at temperatures down to -15°C/5°F; needs no winter protection

**DROUGHT TOLERANCE** Poor

**PROBLEMS** Aphids, caterpillars, leafhoppers and vine weevil; bud blast, honey fungus, powdery mildew, rust and silver leaf

**CARE** Remove dead, diseased or damaged material; grows into a shapely plant unaided

**PROPAGATION** Semi-ripe cuttings in late summer; layering in autumn

**GREENFINGER TIP** *Never plant rhododendrons deeper than the depth of the pot*

# Ribes odoratum
## Buffalo currant

⬆ 2m/6ft ⬌ 2m/6ft                    **EASY**

This deciduous shrub with a spreading habit comes from the USA and is a departure from the usual flowering currants, which have pinky red flowers and foliage that smells of musky blackcurrant. It offers both fragrance and fine foliage, with appealing, light green lobed leaves. From mid-spring, clusters of bright yellow, clove-scented star-shaped flowers emerge from tubular red flower buds just as the leaves start unfurling, and the stamens and reverse of the petals can often be tinted red too. Small, round berries follow the flowers.

**BEST USES** Ideal for the cottage garden; works well as informal flowering hedging; good for the wildlife garden; makes an appealing wall shrub

**FLOWERS** April to May

**ASPECT** Any, in a sheltered or exposed position; full sun to partial shade

**SOIL** Any fertile, moist, well-drained soil

**HARDINESS** Fully hardy at temperatures down to -15°C/5°F; needs no winter protection

**DROUGHT TOLERANCE** Excellent, once established

**PROBLEMS** Aphids; coral spot, honey fungus and powdery mildew

**CARE** Trim lightly after flowering, cutting spent flowering stems to bushy new growth lower down or to the nearest strong buds

**PROPAGATION** Hardwood cuttings in winter

## *Rosa* 'Maigold' ♉

⬆ 2.5m/8ft ⬌ 2.5m/8ft                    **EASY**

This vigorous, modern hybrid climbing rose is one of the earliest roses to flower, and has quite good disease resistance. It has a fairly upright, untidy growing habit, with glossy deep green leaves; the stems are ultra-prickly, throwing out clusters of very showy, extravagant, semi-double coppery yellow flowers (up to 10cm/4in across) that are deeply fragrant. It sends out a few more blooms in early autumn, once its main flowering is over.

**BEST USES** An energetic climber for pergolas and arbours, or trained along a sunny wall; also does well on a north-facing wall

**FLOWERS** May to June

**ASPECT** Any, in a sheltered position; full sun to partial shade (but flowering is reduced in shade)

**SOIL** Any fertile, humus-rich, moist, well-drained soil

**HARDINESS** Fully hardy at temperatures down to -15°/5°F; needs no winter protection

**DROUGHT TOLERANCE** Excellent, once established

**PROBLEMS** Aphids, caterpillars, leafhoppers and scale insects; blackspot, downy and powdery mildew, honey fungus, rose ball, rose soil sickness and rust

**CARE** Mulch with organic matter in late winter or early spring; remove dead, diseased or damaged wood in late autumn or early spring; deadhead (where practical); for pruning, see pages 36–7

**PROPAGATION** Hardwood cuttings in autumn

## *Rosa xanthina* 'Canary Bird' ♉

⬆ 3m/10ft ⬌ 4m/13ft                    **EASY**

A modern rose of Asian origin, this finely arching, low-growing shrub rose is one of the earliest to flower, from spring into summer. Growing far wider than it is tall, it has pliable, reddish brown stems, and the slightly unusual, matt, ferny, mid-green leaves provide a charming backdrop to the very pretty, single, saucer-shaped, five-petalled pale primrose yellow flowers with pronounced golden stamens that are lightly apple-scented.

**BEST USES** Excellent as a small climber, an informal hedge or grown up low brick walls

**FLOWERS** May

**ASPECT** Any, in a sheltered or exposed position; full sun to partial shade (flowering will be reduced in shade)

**SOIL** Any fertile, moisture-retentive soil

**HARDINESS** Fully hardy at temperatures down to -15°C/5°F; needs no winter protection

**DROUGHT TOLERANCE** Excellent, once established

**PROBLEMS** Aphids, caterpillars, leafhoppers and scale insects; blackspot, downy and powdery mildew, honey fungus, rose ball, rose soil sickness and rust

**CARE** Mulch with organic matter in late winter or early spring; remove any dead, diseased, damaged, crossing or weak growth in late autumn or early spring; deadhead spent blooms (where practical); for pruning, see pages 36–7

**PROPAGATION** Hardwood cuttings in autumn

## *Akebia quinata*
### Chocolate vine

⬆ 12m/40ft ⬌ 3m/10ft **EASY**

This semi-evergreen climber from Asia makes energetic, rapid growth and offers superb flower and foliage. The multi-lobed fresh green leaves are appealing in their own right, with the bonus of vanilla-scented, cupped, plummy chocolate flowers with distinctive pale rose-coloured stamens, borne in slightly pendent clusters on smooth, slender, short branching stems. Curious damson-coloured seed pods follow the flowers, revealing silver white seeds when they ripen and split open in autumn.

> **BEST USES** Ideal for growing over pergolas, along fencing or through larger trees and shrubs

**FLOWERS** March to April

**ASPECT** Any, in a sheltered position; full sun to partial shade (but flowering is reduced in shade)

**SOIL** Any fertile, moist, well-drained soil

**HARDINESS** Fully hardy at temperatures down to -15°C/5°F; needs no winter protection

**DROUGHT TOLERANCE** Poor

**PROBLEMS** None

**CARE** Trim lightly after flowering, and remove any dead, diseased or damaged wood; protect young plants from cold and frost

**PROPAGATION** Layering in late autumn/winter and early spring

**GREENFINGER TIP** *Ensure this has sturdy supports from the outset as it can get quite heavy*

## *Clematis armandii*

⬆ 8m/26ft ⬌ 4m/13ft **EASY**

Once again, we have China to thank for this most elegant twining evergreen climber, which is vigorous and fast-growing (so you will need to keep up with tying in new growth). The unusual foliage has long, narrow, strap-like leaves of deep polished green which is slightly bronzed when juvenile. The fat, creamy flower buds burst open to release a rich almond fragrance from the creamy white, star-shaped four-petalled flowers that literally smother the plant in spring and make it an opulent scented addition to the garden.

> **BEST USES** Ideal growing over an archway or on a large house wall, where the fragrance can waft through open windows

**FLOWERS** March to April

**ASPECT** South or west facing, in a sheltered position with protection from cold winds; full sun

**SOIL** Any fertile, moist, well-drained soil

**HARDINESS** Frost hardy at temperatures down to -5°C/23°F; needs winter protection

**DROUGHT TOLERANCE** Poor

**PROBLEMS** Aphids, caterpillars and earwigs; clematis wilt

**CARE** Trim lightly after flowering, removing dead, diseased or damaged wood; if it gets too unruly, cut back fairly hard in late winter or early spring

**PROPAGATION** Internodal semi-ripe cuttings in mid to late summer; layering from late summer to early autumn

## *Drimys winteri* 🏅
### Winter's bark

⬆ 15m/50ft ⬌ 10m/32ft       **EASY**

This evergreen shrub from South America is an energetic plant and offers gardeners a triple dose of fragrance. It forms an upright tree, densely clothed in handsome, elliptical, leathery, deep green leaves (some 8cm/3in long) that are pepper-scented and held on red-flushed stems. The bark of the tree is aromatic and the small clusters of twenty or so prettily star-shaped creamy white flowers (flushed pink when tight in bud) are jasmine-scented. The flowers are produced at the tips of the branches.

> **BEST USES** Ideal for formal gardens and shrubberies or in large containers; does well in a warm, sunny position at the base of a wall or in a sheltered sunny courtyard

**FLOWERS** April to June

**ASPECT** South, west or east facing, in a sheltered position with protection from cold winds; full sun to partial shade

**SOIL** Any fertile, moist, well-drained soil

**HARDINESS** Frost hardy at temperatures down to -5°C/23°F; needs winter protection

**DROUGHT TOLERANCE** Poor

**PROBLEMS** None

**CARE** Remove dead, diseased or damaged material after flowering

**PROPAGATION** Semi-ripe cuttings in summer

## *Illicium anisatum*
### Chinese star anise

⬆ 8m/26ft ⬌ 6m/20ft       **EASY**

This slow-growing Chinese evergreen shrub has a conical habit with aromatic leaves and perfumed flowers. It is easy to grow (if your soil is on the acid side) and offers year-round interest. The oval, leathery, glossy dark green leaves (about 13cm/5in long) smell of aniseed when crushed, and small, rounded, creamy flower buds are clustered at the tips of the smooth, strong, green stems. The buds open to reveal small, spidery, slightly nodding, creamy white flowers (about 2.5cm/1in across) with a spicy scent.

> **BEST USES** Adds structure to a lightly shaded formal garden or courtyard; does well in large containers on city patios; good for culinary use

**FLOWERS** March to May

**ASPECT** South, west or east facing, in a sheltered position; full sun to partial shade

**SOIL** Any fertile, humus-rich, moist, well-drained acid soil

**HARDINESS** Frost hardy at temperatures down to -5°C/23°F; needs winter protection

**DROUGHT TOLERANCE** Poor

**PROBLEMS** None

**CARE** Minimal pruning, removing dead, diseased or damaged wood as needed

**PROPAGATION** Semi-ripe cuttings in summer

**GREENFINGER TIP** *For a nicely rounded topiary shrub, nip out the central pointed stem regularly*

# HONEYSUCKLES

Honeysuckles (*Lonicera*) abound across the northern hemisphere and are climbers or bushy shrubs. Some are evergreen, others are deciduous, but most are fully hardy. There are numerous scented varieties, but a few have no perfume at all, so check that you are buying a fragrant plant. The fragrant choices have pretty tubular flowers in pinks, oranges, yellows and whites. Some enjoy basking in full sun in hot, dry spots with well-drained soil, while the woodland climbers thrive happily in moist soil with a certain degree of shade. They are low maintenance plants, with both climbers and shrubs needing nothing more than a light trim after flowering, although established climbers benefit from a winter or early spring prune, removing a third of the flowering shoots.

Exceptionally fragrant climbing varieties include the fully hardy *Lonicera periclymenum* (7m/22ft × 1.5m/5ft) – *see above* – with creamy yellow flowers, sometimes streaked red, in July and August, and *L.p.* 'Belgica' and *L.p.* 'Graham Thomas' ℣, both with white flowers ageing to yellow. Evergreen *L.* × *heckrottii* (5m/16ft) has satsuma orange and yellow fragrant flowers in summer.

For the best perfumes shrub-wise, opt for *L. fragrantissima* (see page 84), *L.* × *purpusii* 'Winter Beauty' ℣ (see page 84) and *L. standishii* 'Budapest' (2m/6ft), a compact semi-evergreen shrub with fragrant white flowers, edged ice pink, from late winter to early spring.

## *Lonicera japonica* 'Halliana' ℣
### Hall's honeysuckle

⬆ 10m/32ft ↔ 3m/10ft      **EASY**

This Japanese evergreen twining climber is one of the earliest of the climbing honeysuckles to flower, providing foliage, gentle colour and perfume for a great length of time. It is fast-growing, with tapering, oval, mid-green leaves, and produces masses of honey-scented tubular pale lemon and white flowers, which mature to dark yellow. Polished, black berries often appear in autumn, attracting scavenging birds. *L.j.* 'Dart's World' has fragrant red and white flowers; *L.j.* 'Aureoreticulata' has marbled gold leaves with creamy yellow/white flowers.

> **BEST USES** A natural choice for the cottage or wildlife garden; ideal for screening ugly walls and fences; good for coastal gardens

**FLOWERS** April to August

**ASPECT** Any, in a sheltered or exposed position; full sun to partial shade

**SOIL** Any fertile, humus-rich, moist, well-drained soil

**HARDINESS** Fully hardy at temperatures down to -15°C/5°F; needs no winter protection

**DROUGHT TOLERANCE** Good, once established

**PROBLEMS** Powdery mildew

**CARE** Mulch annually in early spring; remove dead, diseased or damaged material after flowering

**PROPAGATION** Layering in spring; semi-ripe cuttings in summer

## Schisandra rubriflora

⬆ 10m/32ft ⬌ 6m/20ft       **EASY**

This deciduous woody-stemmed twining climber from Asia is one of my favourite climbers, being elegant and easy to grow, with great flowers, scent and shape. It has appealing ruby red stems and elliptical dark green leaves that really show off the simple, cup-shaped, vivid, deep carmine red flowers (2.5cm/1in across) which hang in fragrant clusters in spring. As if that weren't enough, waxy red berries are produced if the plant is pollinated (but you need to grow one male and one female plant to get the berries). My daughter describes it as Christmas-on-a-stem!

> **BEST USES** Does well trained against a formal wall or house front; excellent for the wildlife and woodland garden; ideal for a shady city garden

**FLOWERS** May to June

**ASPECT** South, west or east facing, in a sheltered position with protection from cold winds; full sun to partial shade

**SOIL** Any fertile, humus-rich, moist, well-drained soil

**HARDINESS** Fully hardy at temperatures down to -15°C/5°F; needs no winter protection

**DROUGHT TOLERANCE** Poor

**PROBLEMS** None

**CARE** Minimal pruning in late winter or early spring, removing unwanted growth and dead, diseased or damaged material; tie in young shoots to establish a good framework in the first two years

**PROPAGATION** Layering in autumn or winter

## Stauntonia hexaphylla

⬆ 9m/30ft ⬌ 2.5m/8ft       **EASY**

Some of the loveliest climbers come from Asia and this energetic, evergreen twining climber is one such gift. It has elliptical deep green fingers for leaves (up to 15cm/6in long) and clusters of hanging pale green stems, each drooping with a single, belled, flare-edged flower that is snowy white, stained violet at the base, and exotically perfumed. The flowers may be small at only 2cm/¾in across at best, but they pack a delightful perfumed punch, which you can smell some distance away before realising that the tiny restrained flowers are responsible for the lovely whiff. Purple berries follow the flowers.

> **BEST USES** Best against a sunny, sheltered wall or sited in a warm, light courtyard; grow through a winter-flowering shrub that needs enhancing; ideal for cottage and wildlife gardens

**FLOWERS** April to May

**ASPECT** South or west facing, in a sheltered position; full sun to partial shade (provide shading from midday sun)

**SOIL** Any fertile, moist, well-drained soil

**HARDINESS** Frost hardy at temperatures down to -5°C/23°F; needs winter protection

**DROUGHT TOLERANCE** Poor

**PROBLEMS** None

**CARE** Trim lightly after flowering to maintain size and spread, and remove dead, diseased or damaged material

**PROPAGATION** Semi-ripe cuttings in summer

## *Syringa vulgaris* 'Madame Lemoine' ♈
### Lilac

⬆ 7m/22ft ⬌ 7m/22ft　　　　EASY

Lilacs are a group of European deciduous shrubs famed for their powerfully fragranced flowers in late spring through to summer. This choice variety has appealing fresh green heart-shaped leaves (10cm/4in long), but its winning feature is the upward-stretching heavy plumes of pure white, double flowers (up to 20cm/8in long) that appear at the tips of the branches and are exquisitely perfumed. Bees and butterflies throng among the gorgeous blooms. *S.v.* 'Charles Joly' ♈ has deep lilac flowers; *S.v.* 'Katherine Havemeyer' ♈ has pinky lavender blossoms.

**BEST USES** Ideal for the cottage or wildlife garden; lovely in a 'white' garden or sunny mixed border; attractive to pollinating insects

**FLOWERS** May to June
**ASPECT** Any, in a sheltered or exposed position; full sun
**SOIL** Any fertile, humus-rich, moist, well-drained soil
**HARDINESS** Fully hardy at temperatures down to -15°C/5°F; needs no winter protection
**DROUGHT TOLERANCE** Good, once established
**PROBLEMS** Leaf miners; honey fungus and lilac blight
**CARE** Cut out dead, diseased or damaged material in late winter or early spring
**PROPAGATION** Greenwood cuttings in summer

## *Wisteria sinensis* ♈
### Chinese wisteria

⬆ 15m/50ft ⬌ 12m/40ft　　　　EASY

The emperor of climbers, this vigorous deciduous climber from China is renowned for its perfume and extravagant flowers. Twining stems (which need tying in as they grow) produce slim, straight pendent green flower stems that are hung with fragrant chandeliers of highly perfumed lilac flowers, before the lance-shaped fresh green leaves appear. Long, pendulous, felty, sage green pea pods are produced in number as flowering fades. *W.s.* 'Alba' ♈ has white flowers.

**BEST USES** Excellent to clothe a house front or long tall fence; very pretty as a standard tree

**FLOWERS** May to June
**ASPECT** South or west facing, in a sheltered position; full sun (but flowers reasonably well in partial shade)
**SOIL** Any fertile, moist, well-drained soil
**HARDINESS** Fully hardy at temperatures down to -15°C/5°F; needs no winter protection
**DROUGHT TOLERANCE** Excellent, once established
**PROBLEMS** Frost can damage flower buds, particularly on east-facing walls
**CARE** For pruning, see page 107
**PROPAGATION** Sow seed in early spring; softwood cuttings in spring to mid-summer; hardwood cuttings or layering in winter

**GREENFINGER TIP** *Always buy a grafted wisteria in flower: it can take up to seven years to flower from seed*

# Fragrant roses

Roses seem to come top of every survey as the nation's favourite plant. They offer the gardener different habits from diminutive patio roses to shrubs, climbers and ramblers, and beautiful blooms in a variety of shapes, tremendous colour range and widely diverse floral fragrances.

## Choosing roses

All the roses recommended in this book have fragrant flowers. Trying to categorise the various scents is well nigh impossible. Some are barely fragrant while others offer heavy, intoxicating perfumes. Some are sweetly scented, while others smell spicy or fruity, and the old-fashioned roses possess an opulent, rich, heady perfume. The only way to choose a rose scent is to get your head among the blooms and inhale deeply.

.................................................................................

*Rosa* 'New Dawn' grown over a pergola provides a fragrant walkway

There are all sorts of roses with different shapes and habits to choose from. Climbers and rambling roses are ideal for growing against walls, and along fences, on pergolas and trellis or adorning garden archways, and some of the very large ramblers can be grown through trees or over outhouses. The bush, shrubby and standard roses are useful for formal beds and borders and look fantastic planted in gravel gardens. Some are also ideal as hedges for wildflower gardens and meadows, and the more upright species look great left growing against short pillars and fences. On the smaller side, the patio and miniature roses are ideal for pots and containers, in small borders or fronting the edge of flowerbeds. Ground cover roses are slightly larger (up to 60cm/24in) and have a more spreading habit.

The shapes and style of the blooms differ enormously, too. Some are single, others double-petalled; some flowers are small, others big, loose and blowsy, and they can be goblet-shaped or deeply cupped. Like choosing scent, the choice of flower is a very individual one.

A further difference is that some flower once during the growing season, whereas others put out a modest second flowering after the main flush (these are known as repeat-flowering). And finally, there is a choice of colours, from white and a huge range of pastel pinks through to yellows and rich reds.

## Aspect

Most roses need several hours of sunshine a day to bloom at their best. Some are shade-tolerant, but the blooms aren't so profuse in shady conditions.

There are a few fragrant roses that will thrive on a north wall. These include the modern climber *Rosa* 'Golden Showers' ♛ with honey-scented bright yellow blooms; the climbing rose *R*. 'New Dawn' ♛ with fragrant double pink flowers; the Bourbon rose *R*. 'Zéphirine Drouhin' with fragrant deep cerise flowers and an almost thornless climbing habit; and the climbing Hybrid Teas *R*. 'Climbing Madame Caroline Testout', which has gorgeous soft pink, loose, cabbagey blooms and *R*. 'Climbing Ena Harkness', with double crimson flowers.

## Soil

All roses prefer a rich, well-drained soil, but I have seen roses blooming defiantly on dry-as-dust roadsides in the sunny Mediterranean, which proves that their reputation for being drought tolerant is pretty cast iron. They are very successful even on heavy clay, as long as it has been improved with organic matter to increase the drainage.

## Planting

Planting container-grown roses is simple, and can be done at almost any time of year. Dig a hole a little wider than the pot and

*R*. 'Zéphirine Drouhin' will thrive on a north wall

throw in a handful of well-rotted organic matter; gently remove the plant from the container and place in the hole. (Roses often have a visible knobbly growth, known as the graft union, at their base: make sure this is a good 2.5cm/1in below the soil surface when you plant.) Fill in around the plant with soil, firm it down and water it well.

If you are planting a potted rambler or climber, position the plant about 30cm/12in from the pillar, trellis or wall and angle it towards the structure you intend to grow it against. Backfill as above.

Bare-rooted roses can be bought from nurseries from November to March and are usually much cheaper than container-grown roses, though the choice may not be as wide. They are ideal if you are planning to grow a fragrant rose hedge, or need roses in large numbers. Bare-root roses may dry out in transit, so water them as soon as they arrive. Fan out the roots gently in the bottom of the planting hole and proceed as above.

A word of caution: don't plant roses where other roses have grown in the last three years as this will greatly increase the risk of rose soil sickness (see page 116).

## Training

Most roses don't need training. However, some shrub roses can be a bit sprawly and need supports to help them stay upright, and standard roses, where all the growth is on top of a clear, supporting stem, will need staking (see pages 103–4).

The best way to get a spectacular flowering display from climbers or ramblers is to train the stems horizontally, rather than letting the roses grow upward. Establish a good framework of stems from the start and you can expect more profuse flowering, with an even flowering pattern across the plant instead of all the blooms being at the top, so it is worth taking the time to train them on to a set of wires or other support (see page 104).

*R. 'Golden Showers' clings to its chicken-wire support*

To train a newly planted climbing rose, fan out the upright stems, gently but firmly, spacing them as evenly as possible with the central stems upright, radiating out to more angled and horizontally placed stems (although rose stems are stiff by nature, they are bendy enough when young to allow you to do this). Tie them in to your trellis or wire supports using garden twine or plant ties. In the second and third year, keep tying in the new long stems horizontally to form a basic framework, filling gaps as you go. Follow the same procedure when growing climbing or rambling roses over an arbour, arch or walkway.

## Feeding

Give your roses an annual application of well-rotted manure or other organic matter in spring, or a small handful of rose fertiliser scattered on the soil at the base (and watered in well). This is all the nourishment they need.

## Pests and diseases

The most common pests and diseases you are likely to encounter when growing roses are aphids (especially greenfly), blackspot, rust and mildew. These are dealt with in the section on Problems (see page 110). Roses suffer more from pests and diseases than almost any other plant I can think of, so it is wise to plant disease-resistant varieties whenever possible. Fortunately, there are plenty to choose from.

## Pruning

Pruning prevents roses growing straggly and ensures they bloom as bountifully as possible. There is no simple formula for pruning roses: even rose breeders can't seem to agree on the best way to do it. You will get a feel for it with experience, but here are a few basic pointers.

Roses are usually pruned in spring, from March to early April at the latest, as the buds begin to swell and when (hopefully) the worst of the frosts are over.

First remove the three Ds – dead, diseased or damaged growth – and any crossing or overcrowded stems.

Next remove the suckers. Many roses have been grafted (the top is a named rose, welded to the roots of a wild species). Suckers are the new growth that comes from the base of the plant. They tend to grow more quickly than the rest of the rose, making tall, arching growth that will take over if not kept in check. Twist them and pull them away rather than cut them. Modern and miniature roses are less likely to make suckers.

When a rose is growing very energetically, it is tempting to cut it back hard, but the plant will only grow more strongly in response. For any flowering shrub (including roses), prune lightly for light growth and prune hard to stimulate more vigorous growth.

**Miniature and patio roses** Cut low-growing hedging plants to roughly half their height with shears or a hedgecutter. For taller shrubs, prune back to 4–6 buds.

## MAKING A PRUNING CUT

Using sharp, clean secateurs, make a sloping cut about 1cm/½in above an outward-facing bud (if you cut too close to a bud, the stem will die back and the bud will rot). Slope the cut away from the developing bud so that rainwater will run off the stem, instead of pooling on the bud and rotting it.

When cutting back to a specific number of buds, count your buds from the base of the plant just above the 'union'. Don't be too picky about this, but do remember that you always prune above the bud.

**Ground cover roses** need little pruning: simply cut out some of the older wood when necessary.

**Bush and shrub roses** Remove any stems that are growing in the middle of the plant, so that the centre is left open. This keeps air circulation at its most efficient and helps to reduce mildew, which thrives in cramped conditions.

Cut back new stems to about 25cm/10in above the ground. To encourage new growth in sparse areas of the plant, cut back long shoots by a third of their overall length or short shoots to 3–5 buds.

**Standard roses** Standard (or half-standard) roses tend to be top-heavy and will rock on their stems in strong winter winds. To prevent rocking, prune the top growth back by a third or half each November, when the plant is dormant.

**Climbers and rambling roses** If necessary, prune climbing repeat-flowering roses in spring, and summer-flowering roses immediately after flowering. Ramblers need very little pruning and even the new suckering shoots of non-grafted roses are best left alone. Remove suckering shoots from grafted plants immediately.

If the stems are becoming bare at the bottom, cut back a third of the older or poorly productive stems to just above ground level after flowering. Remove any dead, diseased or damaged plant material that you can reach and cut back any wayward stems. Otherwise, leave them to their own devices. There will come a time when a large climbing or rambling rose is just too high and mighty for pruning to be practical at the top.

# SUMMER

All of the flowering plants and shrubs are lovely, but those that are sweetly perfumed just seem to improve on nature's perfection. Summer-flowering plants offer an enormous colour range, as well as some of the more exotic plant perfumes. The myrrh-enhanced 'welcome home' of a blowsy old-fashioned rose trained around the front porch or the exotic waft of jasmine on the patio can transform your garden. Fragrant plants encourage wildlife to visit, turning the space into a floral-scented sanctuary, awhirl with dizzying butterflies and the soothing droning of bees.

## *Agrimonia eupatoria*
Agrimony/Cocklebur

⬆ 30–60cm/12–24in ⬌ 20–30cm/8–12in **EASY**

This clump-forming rhizomatous hardy perennial, originally from northern temperate regions, can be found growing wild in hedgerows, wasteland and fields. The pointed oval, slightly serrated, bristly dark green leaves have a smell reminiscent of apricots when bruised; if you can be bothered to dig it up, the root emits the same fruity fragrance. The stout, tallish, bristled mid-green stems are studded with green flower buds, which open to small, cheerful, simple, five-petalled, slightly gappy buttercup yellow flowers along their length, which also possess fruity perfume. Hairy, clinging burrs follow the flowers. Agrimony has a long history as a medicinal herb, and has been used to treat everything from liver complaints to backache.

**BEST USES** Excellent for wildflower gardens and lightly shaded woodland borders

**FLOWERS** July to August
**ASPECT** Any, in a sheltered or exposed position; full sun to partial shade
**SOIL** Any fertile, well-drained soil
**HARDINESS** Fully hardy at temperatures down to -15°C/5°F; spring frosts can damage flowering wood
**DROUGHT TOLERANCE** Poor
**PROBLEMS** None
**CARE** Deadhead spent flowers to prevent self-seeding
**PROPAGATION** Division in autumn

## Alstroemeria 'Sweet Laura'
Peruvian lily

⬆ 30cm/12in ↔ 30cm/12in          **EASY**

Alstroemerias are clump-forming tuberous perennials from South Africa that have a reputation for being difficult to grow, with no tolerance for extremes of heat or cold, but this variety should prove easier as it is one of the hardiest, as well as one of the rare fragrant examples. It has the trademark narrow, linear, mid-green pointed leaves that form a pleasing low, leafy, slow-spreading mound, with tall, brown-burgundy, straight, smooth stems supporting branched, lightly fragrant funnel-shaped flowers (up to 5cm/2in across) of deep golden yellow, flushed apricot orange at the tips, and charmingly smattered with maroon speckling.

> **BEST USES** Ideal for cottage gardens and formal borders; well worth a try in pots or containers; excellent as cut flowers

**FLOWERS** July to October
**ASPECT** Any, in a sheltered position; full sun to partial shade
**SOIL** Any fertile, moist, well-drained soil
**HARDINESS** Fully hardy/borderline at temperatures down to -15°C/5°F; may need winter protection in colder areas
**DROUGHT TOLERANCE** Poor
**PROBLEMS** Slugs and snails
**CARE** Plants need staking; remove spent flower stems; protect tubers with a dry mulch in winter
**PROPAGATION** Division in early spring or summer

## ✕ Amarcrinum memoria-corsii

⬆ 90cm/3ft ↔ 60cm/24in          **EASY**

Cross a crinum with a belladonna lily and this gorgeous hybrid is the result. It is a robust evergreen bulbous perennial, which could easily be mistaken for an amaryllis, but is better suited to cooler climes. It has large, tough, strappy, fresh green leaves (up to 60cm/24in long), which don't get as tatty as amaryllis, and characteristic, tall sturdy stems carrying up to ten, delicately scented, loose sprays of rose pink flared trumpets (up to 10cm/4in long). It flowers longer than its rival and is a lovely contrast to the usual muted autumn flower palette of yellow-golds.

> **BEST USES** Grows well among ornamental grasses; ideal for colour in an exotic border; good in pots on a sunny patio or in a conservatory

**FLOWERS** August to October
**ASPECT** South, west or east facing, in a sheltered position; full sun
**SOIL** Any fertile, humus-rich, moist, well-drained soil
**HARDINESS** Frost hardy at temperatures down to -5°C/23°F; needs winter protection
**DROUGHT TOLERANCE** Poor
**PROBLEMS** Aphids, narcissus bulb fly, narcissus eelworms, slugs and snails; red spider mite (indoors)
**CARE** Plant in late summer or spring with the bulb tops just below the soil surface; dry mulch with straw in frost-prone areas
**PROPAGATION** Buy bulbs in summer; offsets in spring (can take two years to reach a good size)

## *Aquilegia fragrans*
### Columbine/Granny's bonnet

⬆ 15–40cm/6–16in ⬌ 15–20cm/6–8in **EASY**

This upright, clump-forming hardy perennial from the Himalayas is almost idiot proof. It has deeply divided lobed leaves of fresh zingy green that form small, neat, scalloped mounds which are appealing even when the plant is not in flower. Each of the tall, smooth, plum-coloured stems is topped with a single, delicate, nodding, spurred creamy white fragrant flower, often tinged mauve, with pronounced yellow-green stamens. The faded flowers are followed by grooved seed cases, which split to allow prolific self-seeding.

**BEST USES** Ideal for cottage and wildflower gardens or a shady woodland garden; suits formal and informal flower borders; does well in pots and containers

**FLOWERS** June

**ASPECT** Any, in a sheltered or exposed position; full sun to partial shade

**SOIL** Any fertile, moist, well-drained soil

**HARDINESS** Fully hardy at temperatures down to -15°C/5°F; needs no winter protection

**DROUGHT TOLERANCE** Poor

**PROBLEMS** None

**CARE** Cut back after flowering to prevent self-seeding

**PROPAGATION** Self-seeds easily; division in early spring (will take time to re-establish)

**GREENFINGER TIP** *Cutting the spent flower stems back will encourage new leafy growth and keep the plant looking good through the year*

## *Caryopteris* x *clandonensis* 'Arthur Simmonds' ♀

⬆ 60cm/24in ⬌ 1.5m/5ft **EASY**

The hardiest of all the caryopteris, this bushy, rounded, deciduous shrub from mountainous areas of Asia is an easy-going plant. It has misty, sage-like grey-green, lightly lavender-scented leaves with silver undersides, making it a fine foliage plant for much of the year. Short, slender, straight reddish flower stems bear pretty soft purple-blue flower spires which are a lure for pollinating insects. When the flowers appear in summer, the pastel colours of the leaves and flowers together give a romantic, misty impression, rather like an abstract watercolour.

**BEST USES** Works well in cottage or formal gardens; ideal for gravel and Mediterranean gardens; use as ground cover to clothe arid banks

**FLOWERS** August to September

**ASPECT** South or west facing, in a sheltered position; full sun

**SOIL** Any fertile, well-drained soil

**HARDINESS** Fully hardy at temperatures down to -15°C/5°F; needs no winter protection

**DROUGHT TOLERANCE** Good, once established

**PROBLEMS** Capsid bugs

**CARE** In spring, cut back to within two leaf buds of the old growth, and remove weak growth from the base

**PROPAGATION** Softwood cuttings in late spring; greenwood cuttings in early summer

## Chlidanthus fragrans
Perfumed fairy lily

⬆ 30cm/12in ↔ 8cm/3in          **MEDIUM**

This frost-tender bulbous perennial from Peru looks and smells exotic from the top of its showy flowers to its slender green 'fairy' toes. It is traditionally grown as a conservatory plant but is worth trying outside in areas with mild winters, in a warm sheltered spot. The narrow, smooth, upright, grey-green leaves are typically bulb-like, and the smooth stems carry multiple flower heads of three to five, large, heavily perfumed golden yellow trumpet-shaped flowers (up to 8cm/3in long).

**BEST USES** Outdoors, plant at the base of a warm wall or in a sunny courtyard; indoors, plant three bulbs in a container (15cm/6in diameter), and use the pot to fill gaps in summer borders

**FLOWERS** June to July

**ASPECT** South, west or east facing, in a sheltered position; full sun to partial shade

**SOIL** Fertile, humus-rich, well-drained sandy soil

**HARDINESS** Frost tender at temperatures below 5°C/41°F; needs winter protection

**DROUGHT TOLERANCE** Poor

**PROBLEMS** None

**CARE** Plant bulbs outdoors 5cm/2in deep and 10cm/4in apart with the nose of the bulb just breaking the soil surface; dry mulch in winter

**PROPAGATION** Offsets in spring

............................................

**GREENFINGER TIP** *As the leaves wither in autumn, try a small dose of potassium sulphate to encourage healthy flower buds the following year*

## Cistus x argenteus 'Peggy Sammons' 🎖
Rock rose

⬆ 90cm/3ft ↔ 90cm/3ft          **EASY**

Rock roses are bushy, spreading, evergreen shrubs and are used to the poor, dry, stony soils of the Mediterranean. The flowers are not scented, but the leaves are. Reliable old 'Peggy' has narrow, pointed, paired, soft, downy sage green leaves. How shall I describe their scent? Honey and amber, perhaps? The hotter the sun, the more potent the fragrance. Slim, lightly branching pastel green stems hold dainty, single, simple, shallow, soft rose pink flowers with golden centres. They look like crumpled tissue paper and only last a day, but are so prolific you will never notice their brevity. C. × a. 'Silver Pink' has silver pink flowers.

**BEST USES** Ideal ground cover for sunny, stony banks or slopes; perfect for the Mediterranean or gravel garden, or against warm, sunny walls

**FLOWERS** July to August

**ASPECT** South or west facing, in a sheltered position; full sun

**SOIL** Any fertile to poor, well-drained soil

**HARDINESS** Frost hardy at temperatures down to -5°C/23°F; needs winter protection

**DROUGHT TOLERANCE** Excellent, once established

**PROBLEMS** None

**CARE** Prune lightly after flowering, removing any dead, diseased or damaged wood

**PROPAGATION** Softwood or greenwood cuttings in summer

## Cosmos atrosanguineus
### Chocolate plant

⬆ 75cm/30in ↔ 45cm/18in          **EASY**

It will come as no surprise to learn that this bushy, clump-forming tuberous tender perennial comes from Mexico – the only country in the world that mixes chocolate and avocado in the kitchen. It does indeed have narrow, oval, pointed avocado green leaves when young, ageing to dark green. Each red-brown stem is topped with dark chocolate brown flower buds, opening to single, simple, deep velvet-textured, chocolate maroon flowers with cocoa-hued centres. The flowers smell of (wait for it . . . ) chocolate.

**BEST USES** Ideal for the Mediterranean or hot-coloured border; pleasing as rich, deep colour in any late-summer garden

**FLOWERS** June to October

**ASPECT** South or west facing, in a sheltered or exposed position; full sun

**SOIL** Any fertile, well-drained soil

**HARDINESS** Frost hardy at temperatures down to -5°C/23°F; needs winter protection

**DROUGHT TOLERANCE** Poor

**PROBLEMS** Aphids, slugs and snails; *Botrytis* (grey mould)

**CARE** Cut back spent flower stems in autumn

**PROPAGATION** Sow seed in situ in spring; basal cuttings in a heated propagator in early spring

## Crinum × powellii 🎖

⬆ 90cm/3ft ↔ 30cm/12in          **EASY**

I inherited a generous forest of this South African bulbous perennial when I moved house years ago and it still ranks as one of my favourites because it has such extravagant flowers. The arching, strap-like, light green leaves are not the main feature, but the tall, smooth, straight, erect, branching stems carry spectacular, rosy pink, lily-scented, flared flower trumpets (about 10cm/4in long) that are captivating from August into early autumn. C. × p. 'Album' 🎖 has white flowers.

**BEST USES** Excellent for bringing vertical form into large late-summer and early autumn borders; clumps up well in containers on a sunny patio

**FLOWERS** August to September

**ASPECT** South, west or east facing, in a sheltered position; full sun

**SOIL** Any fertile, humus-rich, moist, well-drained soil; add organic matter before planting

**HARDINESS** Fully hardy/borderline at temperatures down to -15°C/5°F; may need winter protection in colder areas

**DROUGHT TOLERANCE** Good, once established

**PROBLEMS** None

**CARE** Plant bulbs with the tip just showing above the soil; mulch with organic matter in spring

**PROPAGATION** Pot up rooted offsets in spring

............................................................

**GREENFINGER TIP** *Keep the roots congested and don't divide them too early in their career: they will flower more profusely left undisturbed*

## *Dictamnus albus* var. *purpureus* 🎖
### Burning bush/Purple-flowered dittany

**↑ 90cm/3ft ↔ 60cm/24in**      **EASY**

This slow-growing, clump-forming, woody-based perennial comes from Asia and southern Europe. It needs time to settle down, but is an elegant plant once established, with oval, pointed, light green leaves (about 35cm/14in long). Tall, branching, claret-stained stems with small rosy flower buds open to show the very pretty rosy pink-purple flower spikes, with attractive plum veining. The leaves and flowers are both coated with a flammable oil that is activated by the sun in hot weather, releasing a distinctive citrus scent. The oil will ignite with a match or burning cinder, so keep well away from the barbecue.

**BEST USES** Ideal in hot, sunny borders; also suits cottage gardens and woodland or shady borders

**FLOWERS** May to July

**ASPECT** Any, in a sheltered or exposed position; full sun to partial shade

**SOIL** Any fertile, well-drained soil

**HARDINESS** Fully hardy at temperatures down to -15°C/5°F; needs no winter protection

**DROUGHT TOLERANCE** Excellent, once established

**PROBLEMS** None

**CARE** Cut down to ground level in autumn, or leave foliage to die back in winter

**PROPAGATION** Sow ripe seed immediately in a cold frame; division in spring or autumn

**GREENFINGER TIP** *The roots resent being moved, so apply an organic mulch after division*

## *Disporopsis pernyi*
### Evergreen Solomon's seal

**↑ 40cm/16in ↔ 40cm/16in**      **EASY**

One glance at this Chinese evergreen rhizomatous perennial tells you it is related to both Solomon's seal and lily of the valley. Perhaps it lacks the refinement of either, but it is a compact alternative for year-round foliage cover, spreading by creeping rhizomes. It has paired leaves that are leathery dark green with pronounced vertical veining and sturdy smooth green stems, spotted maroon. The dangling, bell-shaped greenish white flowers have petals that curl outward like peeled fruit. They may not be as dainty as those of the more popular Solomon's seal, but their zesty lemon fragrance more than makes up for this tiny flaw. Rounded blue-black berries follow the flowers.

**BEST USES** Effective ground cover in a woodland garden or shady border; excellent for underplanting in a shrub area with light dappled shade or in a gloomy city patio

**FLOWERS** June

**ASPECT** North, east or west facing, in a sheltered position; partial shade

**SOIL** Any fertile, humus-rich, well-drained soil

**HARDINESS** Fully hardy at temperatures down to -15°C/5°F; needs no winter protection

**DROUGHT TOLERANCE** Poor

**PROBLEMS** None

**CARE** Mulch with organic matter in spring

**PROPAGATION** Division in spring

## *Echinacea* 'Sunset' (Big Sky Series)
**Coneflower**

⬆ 75cm/30in ↔ 60cm/24in     **EASY**

Coneflowers are vigorous, clump-forming perennials from the arid prairies of Central and North America. Originally they were all pinks and purples, but are now available in white, orange, deep and pale pink and all shades in between, although not all are scented. This variety makes strong leafy clumps of lance-shaped, slightly bristly dark green leaves and has tall, sturdy, straight flower stems, each topped with eye-catching, honey-scented salmon pink tubular flowers, lined in soft tangerine, with beautiful deep orange centres, tipped deep red.

**BEST USES** Perfect for bridging the gap between summer and autumn in formal and informal borders; ideal for prairie planting; good for wildflower gardens as bees love this plant

**FLOWERS** July to September
**ASPECT** South or west facing, in a sheltered or exposed position; full sun (tolerant of partial shade but flowering is reduced)
**SOIL** Any fertile, well-drained soil
**HARDINESS** Fully hardy at temperatures down to -15°C/5°F; needs no winter protection
**DROUGHT TOLERANCE** Good, once established
**PROBLEMS** None
**CARE** Deadhead spent flowers to prevent self-seeding
**PROPAGATION** Self-seeds easily; division in spring or autumn

## *Gardenia jasminoides* 'Kleim's Hardy'

⬆ 90cm/3ft ↔ 90cm/3ft     **TRICKY**

Gardenias originate in tropical regions from Africa to Asia and are famed for their rich, exotic fragrance. This variety makes a neat, rounded, compact shrub with polished oval evergreen leaves and shallow salvers of creamy white, highly fragrant flowers with lemon yellow centres. Very slow-growing but free flowering, it is hardier than most and will probably come through a winter outdoors in warm regions, if well sited and protected with fleece; in cold areas, grow it in a pot indoors and move outside in summer.

**BEST USES** Grow in a warm border or in a pot on a sunny patio; indoors, grow in a conservatory in bright light with shading from hot afternoon sun

**FLOWERS** June to July
**ASPECT** South, west or east facing, in a sheltered position with protection from cold winds and frosts; full sun to partial shade
**SOIL** Any humus-rich, moist, well-drained soil
**HARDINESS** Frost tender at temperatures below 5°C/41°F; needs winter protection
**DROUGHT TOLERANCE** Poor
**PROBLEMS** Aphids (whitefly) and mealybugs (indoors); *Botrytis* (grey mould)
**CARE** Mulch with organic matter in spring or feed monthly during growing months; cut out any long shoots growing out of place in spring; indoors, mist the leaves with a water spray
**PROPAGATION** Semi-ripe cuttings in late summer

## Gladiolus murielae 🏅

⬆ 90cm/3ft ⬌ 5cm/2in      **EASY**

I adore *Gladiolus byzantinus* but it is unscented, which leaves the way open for this South African half-hardy bulbous perennial. It has narrow, elegant, upright, blade-like, fresh green leaves, and the graceful wands of gently arching, slender, smooth green stems bear slightly nodding, deeply fragrant pure white funnelled blooms (5cm/2in across) with dark claret throats; the base of each flower is flushed raspberry. The scent is delicious and grows stronger towards evening. It is easy to grow, so if you only have space for one type of summer bulb, make it this one.

> **BEST USES** Ideal for the cottage and wildflower garden or in a formal border; a lovely partner to swaying ornamental grasses

**FLOWERS** August to September

**ASPECT** South, west or east facing, in a sheltered position; full sun

**SOIL** Any fertile, well-drained soil

**HARDINESS** Half hardy at temperatures down to 0°C/32°F; needs winter protection

**DROUGHT TOLERANCE** Poor

**PROBLEMS** Aphids, slugs, snails and thrips; *Botrytis* (grey mould) and gladiolus corm rot

**CARE** In spring, plant corms 15cm/6in deep; after foliage has died, dig up and store over winter in a warm, dry place, or leave in the ground and cover with a thick mulch

**PROPAGATION** Buy fresh corms annually

## Heliotropium arborescens 'Chatsworth' 🏅 Cherry pie

⬆ 45cm/18in ⬌ 45cm/18in      **EASY**

Heliotropiums are a group of evergreen annuals, shrubs and perennials that come from open, dry sandy habitats from the USA to the Canaries. This variety is a tender, short-lived, mounded bushy shrub, often grown as an annual in the UK and used as a highly scented bedding plant. It has oval, pointed, wrinkly, veined deep green leaves and bears tiny, tubular, cherry-scented flowers that form dense, domed flower heads of rich purple. They can grow much taller if given space (around 90cm/3ft). *H.a.* 'Gatton Park' has pale blue flowers, and *H.a.* 'Princess Marina' 🏅 has deep violet flowers.

> **BEST USES** Ideal for the cottage garden or front of borders; excellent as summer ground cover; great in pots; irresistible to butterflies

**FLOWERS** June to August

**ASPECT** South, west or east facing, in a sheltered position; full sun

**SOIL** Any fertile, moist, well-drained soil

**HARDINESS** Half hardy at temperatures down to 0°C/32°F; needs winter protection or grow as annual

**DROUGHT TOLERANCE** Poor

**PROBLEMS** Aphids (whitefly) (indoors)

**CARE** Plant outdoors in summer; in autumn, cut back spent flower stems; in winter, bring indoors

**PROPAGATION** Sow seed at 18°C/64°F in a greenhouse in spring; sow outdoors in situ in mid-spring; semi-ripe cuttings in summer

## Hosta 'Honeybells'
**Plantain lily**

⬆ 75cm/30in ⬌ 1.2m/4ft      **EASY**

Hostas originated in Asia but the USA has produced countless new varieties. This strong-growing clump-forming herbaceous perennial makes a generous open mound of large, heart-shaped pale green leaves (up to 30cm/12in long), with marked veins giving the impression each leaf is pleated. In late summer, smooth straight stalks arise from the leafy crowns, each topped with small, bell-shaped lightly honey-scented white to pale lavender flowers. The only real drawback is their non-stop attack by snails and slugs.

**BEST USES** Provides contrasting foliage to taller, upright perennials in formal or informal borders; looks very modern in pots in shady city gardens

**FLOWERS** July to August
**ASPECT** North, east or west facing, in a sheltered position; full sun (shaded from midday sun) to full shade
**SOIL** Any fertile, moist, well-drained soil
**HARDINESS** Fully hardy at temperatures down to -15°C/5°F; needs no winter protection
**DROUGHT TOLERANCE** Poor
**PROBLEMS** Slugs and snails; vine weevil if grown in pots
**CARE** Mulch annually in spring; remove spent flowering stems
**PROPAGATION** Division in early spring

## Linnaea borealis subsp. *americana*
**Twin flower**

⬆ 8cm/3in ⬌ 90cm/3ft      **EASY**

This creeping carpeting evergreen shrub from North America is a natural woodlander that is sadly in decline in the UK, but really is too delightful to be lost. It has small, rounded, shiny dark green leaves with paler undersides (about 2cm/¾in long). Wiry red stems stand proud of the basal growth, each one topped with twin tubular, dainty, nodding, belled pale pink almond-scented flowers, a little smaller than the leaves, creating a delightful pinky froth. *L. borealis* has larger leaves but slightly smaller pink flowers.

**BEST USES** Ideal ground cover on awkward slopes and banks; perfect for woodland gardens or in a shady city courtyard or patio

**FLOWERS** July to August
**ASPECT** Any, in a sheltered or exposed position; partial shade
**SOIL** Any fertile, humus-rich, moist, well-drained acid soil
**HARDINESS** Fully hardy at temperatures down to -15°C/5°F; needs no winter protection
**DROUGHT TOLERANCE** Poor
**PROBLEMS** None
**CARE** None
**PROPAGATION** Softwood cuttings in summer; dig up rooted runners and pot up

**GREENFINGER TIP** *They flower more profusely in shady conditions, so avoid planting them where they are exposed to overhead bright light*

## Lunaria rediviva
**Perennial honesty**

⬆ 90cm/3ft ⬌ 30cm/12in **EASY**

This hardy herbaceous perennial from Europe to Russia is widely grown for its bushy, clump-forming habit. The toothed, triangular leaves are apple green when young, ageing to dark green, and it has tall, strong, branching stems that are topped with loose clusters of small, star-shaped, lilac-scented pale lavender-hued flowers, from late spring to summer. The flowers are an irresistible lure to pollinating insects and are followed by unmistakable, ghostly, papery pennies (up to 8cm/3in across), which are popular with flower arrangers.

**BEST USES** A reliable plant for the shady border or woodland garden; ideal for wildflower gardens; excellent as a dried flower

**FLOWERS** May to August

**ASPECT** Any, in a sheltered or exposed position; full sun to partial shade

**SOIL** Any fertile, moist, well-drained soil

**HARDINESS** Fully hardy at temperatures down to -15°C/5°F; needs no winter protection

**DROUGHT TOLERANCE** Poor

**PROBLEMS** Aphids; clubroot and white blister

**CARE** Remove spent flower stems to prevent self-seeding; or leave the skeletal seed heads to add shapely autumn interest

**PROPAGATION** Sow seed in spring in a pot or seedbed; division in early spring

## Lupinus 'Noble Maiden' (Band of Nobles Series) Lupin

⬆ 90cm/3ft ⬌ 75cm/30in **MEDIUM**

Unlike the shrubby tree lupins, these garden hybrids, related to the pea family, are clump-forming woody-based perennials with bushy, fresh green, deeply divided palmate leaves and tall, elegant, single-colour or two-tone flower spikes, made up of small pea-like flowers studded closely together to form erect floral steeples. Their scent is very distinctive: a clean, peppery, pea-and-moss perfume unlike any other. This fragrant variety has creamy white flowers.

**BEST USES** An elegant addition to the informal or cottage garden; good for coastal gardens

**FLOWERS** June

**ASPECT** South, west or east facing, in a sheltered position; full sun to partial shade

**SOIL** Any fertile, well-drained, slightly acid soil

**HARDINESS** Fully hardy at temperatures down to -15°C/5°F; needs no winter protection

**DROUGHT TOLERANCE** Poor

**PROBLEMS** Lupin aphid, slugs and snails; powdery mildew

**CARE** May need staking; deadhead to encourage a modest second flowering; remove spent flower spikes if leaves are tatty or mildewed

**PROPAGATION** Basal stem cuttings in mid to late spring

**GREENFINGER TIP** *Lupin aphid can decimate a plant in days, so be vigilant*

## Matthiola incana
### Wild stock

⬆ 80cm/32in ⬌ 40cm/16in  **EASY**

These borderline hardy perennials from across central and southern Europe tend to be short-lived and are often grown as biennials (and the multi-coloured cultivars are best grown as annuals). They have an upright habit with soft, sappy, grey-green leaves on short, lush stems studded with dense clusters of charmingly crumpled petals, forming spikes of double, clove-scented pinkish purple or white flowers. They can suffer from frequent fungal attacks, but this is a small price to pay for their wonderful scent.

**BEST USES** Ideal in a cottage or wildlife garden or informal border; good in pots and containers

**FLOWERS** May to July

**ASPECT** Any, in a sheltered or exposed position; full sun

**SOIL** Any fertile, moisture-retentive soil

**HARDINESS** Fully hardy/borderline at temperatures down to -15°C/5°F; may need winter protection in colder areas

**DROUGHT TOLERANCE** Poor

**PROBLEMS** Aphids, cabbage root fly and flea beetles; *Botrytis* (grey mould), clubroot, powdery mildew, stem and root rots and white blister

**CARE** Mulch annually in early spring; deadhead spent flowers to prevent self-seeding (I am told removing the seed heads improves longevity)

**PROPAGATION** Self-seeds easily; sow seed at 10–18°C/50–64°F in early spring (seedlings prone to damping off); sow outdoors in situ in spring

## Oenothera caespitosa
### Evening primrose

⬆ 20cm/8in ⬌ 20cm/8in  **EASY**

Born in the USA this clump-forming dwarf herbaceous perennial has long, notched, grey-green leaves and short, smooth green-reddish stems, each holding a large, single, bowl-shaped creamy white fragrant flower, fading to pale pink as it matures, with spidery lemon stamens. The perfume, which is released as evening approaches, is undoubtedly the sweetest and most pronounced of all the species. *O. speciosa* (30cm/12in × 30cm/12in) has fragrant, veined, pink and white clustered flowers; if you would like a lemony perfume and bolder colour, opt for the tall, bright yellow scented salvers of *O. biennis* (1.5m/5ft × 60cm/24in).

**BEST USES** Ideal for a dry, sunny spot in a Mediterranean or gravel garden, in troughs or a raised bed

**FLOWERS** July to October

**ASPECT** South, west or east facing, in a sheltered or exposed position; full sun

**SOIL** Any poor, well-drained soil

**HARDINESS** Fully hardy at temperatures down to -15°C/5°F; needs no winter protection

**DROUGHT TOLERANCE** Good, once established

**PROBLEMS** Slugs and snails; powdery mildew

**CARE** Cut back flower stems after flowering

**PROPAGATION** Self-seeds easily; division in early spring; sow seed in pots in a cold frame in spring or summer

## *Paeonia* 'Eden's Perfume'
Peony

⬆ 75cm/30in ↔ 60cm/24in · · · · · · · · · · **EASY**

Peonies are clump-forming herbaceous perennials (and sometimes shrubs) from Europe and Asia. They are the glamorous showgirls of the late-spring to summer garden, adding long-lasting foliar texture and elegance to any border. This strong-growing variety has deeply divided mid-green leaves and smooth red stems, bearing very large, fat flower buds. The bowl-shaped, highly perfumed double flowers (up to 13cm/5in across) are an extravagant confection of shell pink petals, often frilled at the edges, which are flushed apple blossom pink and white.

**BEST USES** Adds impact to a cottage garden or city patio; this variety flowers longer than most so suits containers and borders; great as cut flowers

**FLOWERS** May to July

**ASPECT** South, west or east facing, in a sheltered position; full sun

**SOIL** Any fertile, well-drained soil

**HARDINESS** Fully hardy at temperatures down to -15°C/5°F; needs no winter protection

**DROUGHT TOLERANCE** Poor

**PROBLEMS** Eelworms; *Botrytis* (grey mould), honey fungus and peony wilt

**CARE** Mulch the base in spring; may need staking; deadhead spent flowers

**PROPAGATION** Division in spring or autumn; root cuttings in winter

## *Patrinia triloba* var. *palmata*

⬆ 30cm/12in ↔ 10cm/4in · · · · · · · · · · **EASY**

This clump-forming perennial from Japan isn't widely grown but is very handy for damp, gloomy problem spots. Undemanding and easy to grow, it has deeply divided mid-green leaves like the palms of the hand (up to 10cm/4in across), held on spreading, slightly arching pink stems. Tall, slender, smooth pink-tinted branching stems hold sprays of tiny, sunshine yellow, star-shaped sweetly scented flowers high above the foliage in late summer. *P. triloba* looks almost identical, but has longer flower spurs and is taller (up to 50cm/20in).

**BEST USES** Excellent ground cover on slopes; ideal for woodland gardens, shady borders and gloomy city courtyards; perfect around ponds

**FLOWERS** July to September

**ASPECT** Any, in a sheltered or exposed position; partial to full shade

**SOIL** Any fertile, humus-rich, moist soil

**HARDINESS** Fully hardy at temperatures down to -15°C/5°F; needs no winter protection

**DROUGHT TOLERANCE** Poor

**PROBLEMS** Slugs and snails like to nibble young growth

**CARE** None

**PROPAGATION** Sow ripe seed immediately in pots in a cold frame; division in spring

## *Phlox paniculata* 'White Admiral' ♥
### Perennial phlox

⬆ 90cm/3ft ⬌ 90cm/3ft                **EASY**

Originating in North America, phlox are bushy herbaceous perennials that may be low-growing or tall. They are easy to grow and are valued for their delicious perfume, smart, reliable foliage and wide colour palette. The elliptical, divided leaves look good for much of the year, and the tall, slender, strong stems carry trussed domes of simple, sweetly scented pure white flowers. *P.p.* 'Eventide' ♥ (60cm/24in) has rich purple flowers; *P.p.* 'Miss Pepper' (60cm/24in) has candy pink flowers.

**BEST USES** Perfect in any formal or informal flower border; ideal for bridging the summer–autumn flowering gap; excellent as cut flowers

**FLOWERS** July to October

**ASPECT** South, west or east facing, in a sheltered or exposed position; full sun to partial shade

**SOIL** Any fertile, well-drained soil

**HARDINESS** Fully hardy at temperatures down to -15°C/5°F; needs no winter protection

**DROUGHT TOLERANCE** Poor

**PROBLEMS** Eelworms; leaf spot and powdery mildew

**CARE** Mulch annually in spring; may need staking; deadhead fading flowers to encourage new growth; cut down to ground level in winter

**PROPAGATION** Division in spring or autumn; sow ripe seed in pots in a cold frame in spring

## *Phuopsis stylosa* 'Purpurea'
### Caucasian crosswort

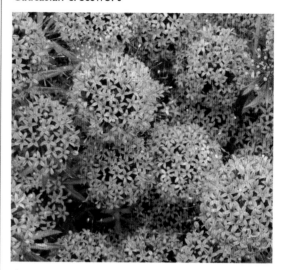

⬆ 20cm/8in ⬌ 50cm/20in              **EASY**

This semi-evergreen, low-growing herbaceous perennial from the Caucasian mountains is low maintenance and problem free, making it a great choice for the novice. It forms a dense matting of narrow, linear mid-green leaves that are muskily aromatic and smell (to me at least) like cold baked beans. It sends up short, branching stems, each topped with a purple-pink drumstick head, comprising a myriad of tiny, sweet-smelling tubular flowers. The two scents don't exactly enhance each other, but you try picking the flowers without bruising the leaves. Still, it's a great little doer.

**BEST USES** Reliable in troughs, containers, at the front of a border or left to tumble over stone walls; good ground cover on banks and slopes

**FLOWERS** July to September

**ASPECT** Any, in a sheltered or exposed position; full sun to partial shade

**SOIL** Any fertile, moist, well-drained soil

**HARDINESS** Fully hardy at temperatures down to -15°C/5°F; needs no winter protection

**DROUGHT TOLERANCE** Excellent, once established

**PROBLEMS** None

**CARE** Cut back after flowering to encourage dense foliage

**PROPAGATION** Division in spring to early summer; semi-ripe cuttings in summer; sow seed in pots in a cold frame in autumn

## Rosa Kent 🎖

⬆ 45cm/18in ⬌ 90cm/3ft          **EASY**

This 'ground cover' rose is only lightly fragranced, lacking the depth of perfume of other roses. It has dense foliage and a neat, tidy, low-spreading repeat-flowering habit with glossy dark green oval leaves. Generous trusses of dainty, blossom-like, semi-double, lightly scented white blooms with yellow centres are followed by shapely, small red rose hips in autumn. It bears up well to all weather, but I'm not convinced that ground cover roses work well as weed-suppressors (and weeding between the thorny stems is not easy).

**BEST USES** Ideal for a cottage garden or in pots and containers on a sunny patio or roof terrace

**FLOWERS** June to September
**ASPECT** Any, in a sheltered position; full sun
**SOIL** Any fertile, humus-rich, moist, well-drained soil
**HARDINESS** Fully hardy at temperatures down to -15°C/5°F; needs no winter protection
**DROUGHT TOLERANCE** Excellent, once established
**PROBLEMS** Aphids, caterpillars, leafhoppers and scale insects; blackspot, downy and powdery mildew, honey fungus, rose ball, rose soil sickness and rust
**CARE** Mulch with organic matter in late winter or early spring; deadhead spent blooms; for pruning, see pages 36–7
**PROPAGATION** Hardwood cuttings in autumn

## Rosa Regensberg

⬆ 40cm/16in ⬌ 50cm/20in          **MEDIUM**

Patio or miniature roses are generally the least fragrant of the roses, but this short floribunda patio rose is an exception. It has a compact, bushy habit with thorny stems and typical small, saw-edged bronze-green glossy foliage. Very free flowering, it produces generous clusters of heavily fragrant dark to lighter pink double blooms (up to 10cm/4in across), with white splashes and gold stamens. A second flush appears in September, after the main crop in summer. It is unusually prone to pests and diseases, but the fragrance takes some beating.

**BEST USES** Good at the front of borders or as low hedging or edging in the cottage, informal or formal rose garden; ideal in pots and containers

**FLOWERS** July, with a second flush in September
**ASPECT** South or west facing, in a sheltered or exposed position; full sun
**SOIL** Any fertile, well-drained soil
**HARDINESS** Fully hardy at temperatures down to -15°C/5°F; needs no winter protection
**DROUGHT TOLERANCE** Excellent, once established
**PROBLEMS** Aphids, caterpillars, leafhoppers and scale insects; blackspot, downy and powdery mildew, honey fungus, rose ball, rose soil sickness and rust
**CARE** Mulch annually with organic matter in late winter or early spring; deadhead spent blooms; for pruning, see pages 36–7
**PROPAGATION** Hardwood cuttings in autumn

## Scabiosa atropurpurea
Pincushion flower/Sweet scabious

⬆ 90cm/3ft ⬌ 20cm/8in                                    **EASY**

Just because a plant is commonplace does not mean it is undesirable and this bushy biennial or hardy annual of Mediterranean origin is a simple joy with a delightful scent. It has tall, wiry green stems arising from oblong basal growth, with sparser feathery leaves further up the stems, each topped with a flattish, slightly domed, pincushion-like fragrant flower (some 5cm/2in across) in pastel lilac. These seem to float above the delicate foliage in a soft lavender haze. Its only drawback is that it can be short-lived, but it self-seeds freely so new plants are easily had.

**BEST USES** Good for naturalising in wildflower meadows, in the Mediterranean garden and in formal or cottage gardens; irresistible to butterflies and bees; good as cut flowers

**FLOWERS** July to September
**ASPECT** South or west facing, in a sheltered or exposed position; full sun
**SOIL** Any fertile, well-drained soil
**HARDINESS** Fully hardy at temperatures down to -15°C/5°F; needs no winter protection
**DROUGHT TOLERANCE** Excellent, once established
**PROBLEMS** None
**CARE** Deadhead spent flowers for further flowering; cut back to ground level in autumn
**PROPAGATION** Division in spring; self-seeds easily; sow seed in situ in mid-spring or sow ripe seed immediately in pots in a cold frame

## Spartium junceum ♀
Spanish broom

⬆ 30cm/12in ⬌ 30cm/12in                                  **EASY**

Here is a Mediterranean shrub that looks good for two thirds of the year and has a sweet fragrance too. You often see them by the roadside in Spain and Italy, covered in dust, so they obviously thrive on paucity. This tidy, upright, deciduous shrub with vivid deep green linear foliage is smothered in sweetly scented, bright yellow pea-like flowers (2.5cm/1in long) from early summer well into autumn. A member of the pea family, it fixes nitrogen in the soil, so it improves the borders as well as making them look good.

**BEST USES** Excellent for coastal gardens or exposed windy sites; a handsome addition to the gravel and Mediterranean garden

**FLOWERS** June to September
**ASPECT** South or west facing, in a sheltered or exposed position; full sun
**SOIL** Any fertile, well-drained soil
**HARDINESS** Frost hardy at temperatures down to -5°C/23°F; needs winter protection
**DROUGHT TOLERANCE** Good, once established
**PROBLEMS** Rabbits
**CARE** Trim lightly in early to mid-spring; cut back older straggly plants to ground level in spring
**PROPAGATION** Self-seeds easily; sow seed in a cold frame in autumn or spring

## Verbena rigida ♟

⬆ 60cm/24in ⬌ 40cm/16in          **EASY**

This South American tuberous perennial (sometimes grown as an annual) is dependable and easy to grow. It has a low-growing, sprawling habit but manages to be fairly neat despite its need to spread sideways. It has coarse, narrow, toothed lance-shaped leaves and lax, branching stems in plummy hues, with sparse foliage cover. In summer, it bears domed flower heads (about 5cm/2in across), made up of clusters of tiny, sweetly fragrant star-shaped flowers in deep rich purple. Needless to say, it is a bee trap.

> **BEST USES** Good for the front of an informal border or in any cottage garden; ideal for pollinating insects; plant in pots at the base of sweet peas for a double dose of fragrance

**FLOWERS** June to September
**ASPECT** South or west facing, in a sheltered or exposed position; full sun
**SOIL** Any fertile, moist, well-drained soil
**HARDINESS** Frost hardy at temperatures down to -5°C/23°F; needs winter protection
**DROUGHT TOLERANCE** Excellent, once established
**PROBLEMS** Aphids, leafhoppers, slugs, snails and thrips; powdery mildew
**CARE** Cut back spent flower stems; dry mulch the crown against frosts in colder areas
**PROPAGATION** Division in spring

## Viola cornuta Alba Group ♟
### Horned violet

⬆ 15cm/6in ⬌ 40cm/16in          **EASY**

This Iberian evergreen perennial is a classic cottage garden favourite. It spreads by creeping rhizomes and has oval, fresh mid-green leaves with slightly serrated edges, but its most appealing feature is its abundant cheerful flowering. Masses of dainty, simple, gappy five-petalled pure white, lightly fragranced flowers (about 5cm/2in across) smother the plant non-stop from spring to summer. *V.c.* 'Minor' ♟ has pale lilac/white scented flowers; *V.c.* 'Icy But Spicy' has gorgeous lavender-grey flowers.

> **BEST USES** A natural for the cottage or white-themed garden; ideal in pots and containers; makes good ground cover in a woodland garden

**FLOWERS** May to August
**ASPECT** South, west or east facing, in a sheltered position; full sun to partial shade
**SOIL** Any fertile, well-drained soil
**HARDINESS** Fully hardy at temperatures down to -15°C/5°F; needs no winter protection
**DROUGHT TOLERANCE** Poor
**PROBLEMS** Aphids, slugs, snails and violet leaf midge; rust and powdery mildew
**CARE** Cut back lightly after flowering
**PROPAGATION** Self-seeds easily; division in spring

## Abelia x grandiflora 🎖

⬆ 3m/10ft ⬅➡ 4m/13ft                    **EASY**

This vigorous, rounded evergreen shrub of garden origin is a delight. It has slightly arching branches, densely clothed with oval, polished deep green leaves. From summer into autumn, pliable red stems bear a profusion of pink buds that open to masses of sweetly scented, tubular pinky white flowers. In flower it has an informal appearance and is undoubtedly a very useful, highly fragrant shrub, offering year-round interest, perfume and a reasonably long flowering period. *A. × g.* 'Hopleys' has variegated foliage and *A. × g.* 'Gold Spot' has yellow leaves; both have white-flushed pink flowers.

**BEST USES** Useful as evergreen hedging; ideal for the mixed shrub or perennial border; a lure for pollinating insects

**FLOWERS** June to October

**ASPECT** South or west facing, in a sheltered position; full sun

**SOIL** Any fertile, well-drained soil

**HARDINESS** Frost hardy/borderline at temperatures down to -5°C/23°F; needs winter protection

**DROUGHT TOLERANCE** Good, once established

**PROBLEMS** None

**CARE** Cut back lightly after flowering

**PROPAGATION** Semi-ripe cuttings in summer

## Azara serrata 🎖

⬆ 4m/13ft ⬅➡ 3m/10ft                    **EASY**

This upright evergreen shrub from Chile is well worth consideration for providing year-round interest. It has oval, slightly toothed, polished deep green leaves and bears prolific clusters of small, rich yellow starburst-style blossoms with a fruity scent. Round white berries are sometimes produced after a long hot summer. The flowers can be prone to frost damage, so keep garden fleece at the ready in early spring to protect the developing flower buds, and give it plenty of room when planting: it needs a fair amount of space to do well.

**BEST USES** A lovely plant for both cottage and formal gardens; ideal for adding a splash of colour and evergreen bones to a shady city garden; can be trained as a wall shrub

**FLOWERS** June

**ASPECT** South, west or east facing, in a sheltered position; full sun to partial shade

**SOIL** Any fertile, well-drained soil

**HARDINESS** Frost hardy at temperatures down to -5°C/23°F; needs winter protection

**DROUGHT TOLERANCE** Poor

**PROBLEMS** None

**CARE** Prune lightly after flowering; if grown as a wall shrub, cut back flowered shoots after flowering, to maintain size and shape

**PROPAGATION** Semi-ripe cuttings in summer

## *Buddleja davidii* 'Royal Red' ♍
### Butterfly bush

⬆ 3m/10ft ⬌ 5m/16ft      **EASY**

Attracting a constant traffic of butterflies when in flower, this Chinese deciduous shrub is fast-growing and needs little maintenance. It has an upright habit and arching branches with long, narrowish, lance-shaped, softly bristled sage green leaves which are unremarkable. However, the tiny star-shaped flowers mass together to form pendulous conical swathes (reminiscent of lilac) of rich, purple-red flowers (about 50cm/20in long), opening from the bottom up and held on straight stems that sweep towards the ground once clothed in flowers. It is sweeter scented than most buddlejas. *B.d.* 'Black Knight' ♍ has deep purple flower trusses.

**BEST USES** An obvious choice for a wildflower garden; easy in a mixed shrub border; looks stunning as an informal hedge when in flower

**FLOWERS** July to September

**ASPECT** South, west or east facing, in a sheltered or exposed position; full sun

**SOIL** Any fertile or poor, well-drained soil

**HARDINESS** Fully hardy at temperatures down to -15°C/5°F; needs no winter protection

**DROUGHT TOLERANCE** Excellent, once established

**PROBLEMS** None

**CARE** In spring, cut back hard to within three buds of the main branch framework

**PROPAGATION** Semi-ripe cuttings in summer; hardwood cuttings in winter

## *Calycanthus floridus*
### Allspice

⬆ 2.5m/8ft ⬌ 3m/10ft      **EASY**

This bushy, deciduous, woodland shrub from America isn't seen much, which is rather surprising as its size suits most gardens and it is easy to grow, without being too rampant. It has a rounded habit and somewhat spreading stems, with dense, coarse, oval, fruity-scented deep green leaves, often maturing to yellow come autumn. The cinnamon-scented bark is used as a spice, and the exotic, narrow-petalled, starry, rich maroon flowers, arranged in twin clusters along the stems, smell deliciously of apples, especially on warm evenings. I am told the roots smell of menthol, so that's a lot of scent for your money.

**BEST USES** Lovely in a woodland garden or slightly shaded city garden; ideal for large containers as it is slow-growing

**FLOWERS** June to July

**ASPECT** South, west or east facing, in a sheltered position; full sun to partial shade

**SOIL** Any fertile, well-drained soil

**HARDINESS** Fully hardy at temperatures down to -15°C/5°F; late frosts can damage young leaves

**DROUGHT TOLERANCE** Poor

**PROBLEMS** None

**CARE** Cut back lightly after flowering to maintain size and shape

**PROPAGATION** Layering in autumn

## Cardiocrinum giganteum
Giant Himalayan lily

⬆ 1.5–4m/5–13ft ↔ 45cm/18in          **EASY**

Whenever you see the Latin word *giganteum* in a plant name you can be sure it is going to be a whopper. This bulbous perennial from Chinese woodlands is no exception, with huge, oval, polished deep green leaves (45cm/18in across) at the base. The leaves grow smaller and more sparse towards the top of the very tall, thick, sturdy flower stem. Each stem produces up to twenty large, hanging, flared trumpets of richly fragrant white flowers (up to 35cm/14in long) with pinky plum streaking inside the petals. Rising from among neighbouring foliage plants, this fragrant wonder will draw gasps of admiration and is as easy to grow as border lilies.

**BEST USES** Excellent in lightly shaded or woodland gardens

**FLOWERS** June to August

**ASPECT** South or west facing, in a sheltered position; partial shade

**SOIL** Any fertile, moist, well-drained soil

**HARDINESS** Fully hardy at temperatures down to -15°C/5°F; needs no winter protection

**DROUGHT TOLERANCE** Poor

**PROBLEMS** Aphids

**CARE** Plant bulbs in autumn, with the tips peeping out of the soil; water well in dry periods; mulch annually and apply leafmould each spring

**PROPAGATION** Buy fresh bulbs; remove offsets after flowering and pot up (but these can take up to five years to flower)

## Carpenteria californica 🎖
Tree anemone

⬆ 2m/6ft ↔ 2m/6ft          **EASY**

Commonly found in the California foothills, this sun-lover is a bushy, upright and spreading evergreen shrub, densely clothed in handsome, long, narrow, elliptical, glossy dark green leaves. In summer it is studded with shallow-cupped sweetly fragrant, snow white flowers (up to 8cm/3in across) with distinctive golden stamens that are a lure for pollinating insects. It can be grown as a wall shrub on a sunny wall, where it will grow slightly larger than stated above.

**BEST USES** An appealing plant in an informal or formal garden; good in a large pot (if kept well watered); ideal for the wildlife garden

**FLOWERS** June to July

**ASPECT** Any, in a sheltered position with protection from strong winds; full sun

**SOIL** Any fertile, moist, well-drained soil

**HARDINESS** Frost hardy at temperatures down to -5°C/23°F; needs winter protection

**DROUGHT TOLERANCE** Good, once established

**PROBLEMS** Leaf spot

**CARE** Trim lightly after flowering, removing any dead, diseased or damaged material; every few years, cut out old stems from the base of the plant

**PROPAGATION** Semi-ripe cuttings in summer

**GREENFINGER TIP** *The leaves often turn yellow at the end of summer, and some may be lost in cold winters: this is natural – the plant is not sick*

## Cestrum parqui
### Willow-leaved jasmine

↑ 2m/6ft ⟷ 2m/6ft                    **EASY**

This upright, deciduous, frost-hardy shrub from Chile has a quiet, soothing presence, with its narrow, willow-like, lance-shaped leaves, which make it an appealing foliage plant. Large clusters of tubular, star-shaped, mustard yellow flowers that are sweetly scented by night enhance the restrained foliage; they are lightly malodorous by day. This will grow easily enough in the south-west of England if it is planted in a warm, sheltered sunny site; treat like a herbaceous perennial and cut back hard in spring. In colder areas, grow it indoors in a conservatory or frost-free greenhouse and wheel it outside in summer.

**BEST USES** A must for seaside gardens; also suits Mediterranean or sheltered city gardens; makes an excellent wall shrub

**FLOWERS** July to October

**ASPECT** South, west or east facing, in a sheltered position; full sun to partial shade

**SOIL** Any fertile, moist, well-drained soil

**HARDINESS** Frost hardy at temperatures down to -5°C/23°F; needs winter protection

**DROUGHT TOLERANCE** Poor

**PROBLEMS** Scale insects; leaf spot

**CARE** In spring, cut back to within two leaf buds of old growth, and remove weak growth from the base

**PROPAGATION** Softwood cuttings in summer

## Clematis 'Jan Fopma'

↑ 1.5m/5ft ⟷ 1.5m/5ft                **EASY**

We tend to think of clematis as climbing plants, but there are some lovely herbaceous or 'border' clematis, and this is one of the scented few of that group. Border clematis are scrambling in habit rather than clinging, and this lovely new perennial has mid-green oval leaves and slim, dusky maroon stems holding single, nodding, chocolate-scented, faded damson-coloured flowers (up to 8cm/3in across) whose sepals, edged in pale lilac, are peeled backwards to reveal creamy stamens. *C. integrifolia* 'Rosea' (1.2m/4ft tall) is a scented red variety and *C.* 'Olgae' (90cm/3ft) is royal blue and scented.

**BEST USES** A must in the cottage garden; grow through shrubs past their flowering best; suitable for containers on both sunny and lightly shaded patios or terraces

**FLOWERS** July to August

**ASPECT** Any, in a sheltered position; full sun to partial shade

**SOIL** Any fertile, moist, humus-rich, well-drained soil

**HARDINESS** Frost hardy at temperatures down to -5°C/23°F; needs winter protection

**DROUGHT TOLERANCE** Poor

**PROBLEMS** Earwigs; clematis wilt

**CARE** In February, cut back to about 15cm/6in above ground level, to a strong pair of buds

**PROPAGATION** Layering in late winter to spring

## Clethra alnifolia 'Paniculata' 🎖
### Summer sweet

⬆ 2.5m/8ft ↔ 2.5m/8ft                    **EASY**

Clethras are acid-lovers by nature and should you have lime-free soil, this deciduous, bushy upright shrub originating in the USA is one for you. It has a suckering habit and can become invasive, so keep a watchful eye on unwanted suckers. It has oval, pointed, mid-green leaves with slightly serrated edges. From late summer into early autumn, short green, sturdy stems form upright spires comprising a myriad of tiny white bell-shaped flowers that are very sweetly scented, covering the bush like fragrant candles. Leaves yellow with the approach of autumn and brown seed heads follow the flowers.

**BEST USES** A must in the wildlife garden as it is loved by bees and butterflies; ideal for cottage gardens or shady city borders and woodland

**FLOWERS** August to September
**ASPECT** Any, in a sheltered position; full sun to full shade
**SOIL** Any fertile, moist, humus-rich, well-drained acid soil
**HARDINESS** Fully hardy at temperatures down to -15°C/5°F; needs no winter protection
**DROUGHT TOLERANCE** Poor
**PROBLEMS** None
**CARE** Cut out dead, diseased or damaged wood in winter; dig out suckers, leaving strong shoots to replace any older wood that is cut out
**PROPAGATION** Greenwood cuttings in summer

## Crambe cordifolia 🎖
### Great sea kale

⬆ 2.5m/8ft ↔ 1.5m/5ft                    **EASY**

Every time I see this sizeable, clump-forming perennial, I want to leap with joy. It has tall, slender, wiry, branching green stems and large, toothed, cabbage-like leaves, coarse at the base, that die back as summer goes. The leaves are not particularly appealing but, come summer, masses of tiny white flower buds detonate into a confetti-like explosion of tiny, sweetly scented, foamy white flowers. On a hot summer's day, it looks like a floating cloud of fragrant mist hovering over the border.

**BEST USES** Ideal at the back of an informal sunny border in a large cottage or coastal garden; great in the wildlife garden

**FLOWERS** June to July
**ASPECT** South, west or east facing, in a sheltered position with protection from cold winds; full sun to partial shade
**SOIL** Any fertile, well-drained soil; short-lived on heavy soil
**HARDINESS** Fully hardy at temperatures down to -15°C/5°F; needs no winter protection
**DROUGHT TOLERANCE** Excellent, once established
**PROBLEMS** Slugs and snails may be a nuisance in spring; the leaves grow tatty with age
**CARE** Cut back to ground level in autumn
**PROPAGATION** Sow seed at 10°C/50°F in pots in a cold frame in spring; division in spring; root cuttings in late autumn to winter

## Dregea sinensis
### (formerly *Wattakaka sinensis*)

⬆ 3m/10ft ↔ 4m/13ft          **EASY**

The word *sinensis* after a plant name says that
the plant is of Chinese origin. This evergreen
twining climber is a bit like a hardier *Hoya*, with
oval mid-green leaves (10cm/4in long) that have
softly hairy undersides. All summer long, it
produces short, smooth, green stems bearing
sweetly fragrant clusters of small, simple,
shallow, five-petalled, star-shaped flowers, which
are a pretty pale pink, freckled claret inside.
Curiously jagged-edged, mid-green pea pods
(about 8cm/3in long) follow the flowers.

**BEST USES** Useful for making screens or divisions
in the garden, on warm sunny walls and fences; good
in containers

**FLOWERS** June to July

**ASPECT** South or west facing, in a sheltered position
with protection from cold winds; full sun to partial
shade

**SOIL** Any fertile, well-drained soil

**HARDINESS** Frost hardy at temperatures down to
-5°C/23°F; needs winter protection

**DROUGHT TOLERANCE** Poor

**PROBLEMS** None

**CARE** Prune lightly after flowering to maintain size and
spread; cut out any dead, diseased or damaged wood
in early spring

**PROPAGATION** Stem cuttings in summer to autumn

## Escallonia 'Iveyi' ♉

⬆ 3m/10ft ↔ 3m/10ft          **EASY**

This South American upright evergreen shrub
works hard in the garden, offering year-round
leaf interest and attractive, scented flowers. It has
rounded oval, polished deep green leaves (about
8cm/3in long) that are often red-tinted in cold
snaps and smell like icing sugar when bruised.
From early summer it is studded with fist-sized,
domed clusters of pure white 'cotton buds' that
open to pretty, five-petalled snow white flowers.

**BEST USES** A versatile plant that works well as
hedging or for creating shape and form in a mixed
shrub border; marvellous for attracting bees and
butterflies; good for coastal gardens

**FLOWERS** July to August

**ASPECT** South, west or east facing, in a sheltered
position; full sun

**SOIL** Any fertile, well-drained soil

**HARDINESS** Frost hardy/borderline at temperatures
down to -5°C/23°F; needs winter protection

**DROUGHT TOLERANCE** Poor

**PROBLEMS** None

**CARE** Trim any unsightly shoots lightly to maintain size
and shape in late spring

**PROPAGATION** Semi-ripe cuttings from non-flowering
shoots in late summer; hardwood cuttings in winter

**GREENFINGER TIP** *If you have inherited a large,
unruly plant, cut it back hard in spring*

## Hedychium forrestii
Ginger lily

↑ 1.5m/5ft ↔ 60cm/24in     **EASY**

Ginger lilies are tender to half-hardy herbaceous perennials with thick, creeping rhizomes. This tall, strong-growing variety from the woodlands of China is among the most frost hardy of the species but it still needs a warm, sunny, sheltered border when grown outdoors. It makes a large plant with huge, handsome, stemless, mid-veined green leaves (up to 50cm/20in across), similar to banana leaves. It bears upright, long, green flower buds that open to reveal exotically fragrant white, tubular, orchid-like flowers (up to 50cm/20in long) with striking long white stamens.

> **BEST USES** Adds architectural accents to an exotic garden; thrives in a conservatory or frost-free greenhouse

**FLOWERS** August to September
**ASPECT** South or west facing, in a sheltered position with protection from cold winds; full sun to partial shade
**SOIL** Any fertile, humus-rich, moist, well-drained soil
**HARDINESS** Frost hardy at temperatures down to -5°C/23°F; needs winter protection; frost damages the flowers
**DROUGHT TOLERANCE** Poor
**PROBLEMS** Aphids and red spider mite (indoors)
**CARE** Water regularly when in growth; cut down spent flower stems; protect roots with a thick mulch; in cold areas, grow indoors in pots and move outside once all risk of frost has passed
**PROPAGATION** Division in spring

## Impatiens tinctoria

↑ 2.5m/8ft ↔ 90cm/3ft     **EASY**

This bushy, tuberous perennial from East Africa is in a class of its own. A rapid grower, its oval, dull mid-green, serrated-edged leaves are not especially appealing, but the spurred, orchid-like, highly scented flowers (about 6cm/2½in across) are a knockout: pure white with magenta throats, they are borne on slender stems in magnificent abundance from summer well into autumn.

> **BEST USES** Ideal in a shady woodland garden or gloomy patio; does well in pots or containers in a sheltered city courtyard

**FLOWERS** July to October
**ASPECT** Any, in a sheltered position with protection from cold winds; full sun to partial shade, with shelter from midday sun
**SOIL** Any fertile, humus-rich, moist, well-drained soil
**HARDINESS** Half hardy at temperatures down to 0°C/32°F; needs winter protection
**DROUGHT TOLERANCE** Poor
**PROBLEMS** Aphids and vine weevil (outdoors); aphids (whitefly) and red spider mite (indoors); *Botrytis* (grey mould)
**CARE** Water sparingly in winter; in cold areas, overwinter in a frost-free greenhouse or grow as an annual
**PROPAGATION** Sow seed at 16–18°C/61–64°F in early spring; sow seed outdoors in situ in late spring after all frost risk has passed

# JASMINES

Jasmines are a group of more than two hundred evergreen and deciduous shrubs and climbers from Europe, Africa and Asia. They often have deeply fragrant flowers, and are also famed for their decorative foliage. They are popularly used in borders or trained up trellis, walls and pergolas, and some make very effective decorative hedging.

Many of the hardier varieties are easy to grow, favouring well-drained sunny spots. Grow those that are frost tender in sheltered positions in the garden, with added winter protection, or grow indoors in a conservatory or greenhouse. They enjoy regular watering in the summer months, with regular but minimal pruning, and don't attract many pests or diseases: red spider mite when grown indoors and aphids outdoors.

Jasmines with exceptional fragrance include fully hardy *Jasminum officinale* ♈ (12m/40ft), a deciduous climber with scented white flowers in summer to autumn; *J. polyanthum* ♈ (3m/10ft plus) – *see above* – a half-hardy evergreen climber with deeply fragrant pinky white flowers from late winter (if grown indoors) or from spring into summer outdoors in warm regions; *J. sambac* ♈ (up to 3m/10ft tall), a beautiful evergreen climber with deeply fragrant white flowers that fade to pale pink with age (in cold regions, this is only suitable for growing indoors). Other recommended climbing varieties include the frost-hardy pink-flowered *J. beesianum* (5m/16ft) and the tender *J. azoricum* ♈ (3–5m/10–16ft) with incredibly fragrant waxy white flowers.

## *Jasminum humile* 'Revolutum' ♈
Yellow jasmine

⬆ 1.5m/5ft ⬌ 3m/10ft　　　　**MEDIUM**

This semi-evergreen shrub of Asian origin is an upright, bushy shrub with larger-than-average, narrow, lance-shaped, glossy green leaves. Slender green stems bear generous clusters of sulphur yellow, waxy perfumed flowers (2.5cm/1in across) from spring to autumn. It is nowhere near as hardy as common jasmine, but is definitely one to try in a sheltered, sunny spot in a frost-free region. It should prove fully evergreen in mild areas.

**BEST USES** Makes a lovely wall shrub against a sunny wall or trellis; ideal in a dappled woodland garden; great for pollinating insects

**FLOWERS** May to September
**ASPECT** South or west facing, in a sheltered position with protection from cold winds; full sun to partial shade
**SOIL** Any fertile, well-drained soil
**HARDINESS** Frost hardy at temperatures down to -5°C/23°F; needs winter protection
**DROUGHT TOLERANCE** Poor
**PROBLEMS** Aphids
**CARE** Trim lightly after flowering, cutting spent flower stems to lower, new bushy growth or the nearest strong buds
**PROPAGATION** Semi-ripe cuttings in summer; layering in autumn

## *Laburnum alpinum* 'Pendulum'
### Scotch laburnum

⬆ 2.5m/8ft ⬌ 2.5m/8ft                    **EASY**

Have you always wanted a laburnum, but never had the room? This small, spreading, slightly stiff, weeping deciduous tree from Europe is slow-growing so ideal for smaller spaces. It has plenty of glossy bright green, oval leaves (up to 8cm/3in long), held on graceful weeping branches. From late spring into summer, drooping strings of fragrant bright yellow pea-like flowers hang in tiered splendour (laburnums are often called Golden rain trees for this reason). Poisonous shiny black seeds follow the flowers. Health and safety regulations decree that this is not child friendly, so you won't see it in parks or avenues any more, which is a shame.

> **BEST USES** Great for the wildlife, cottage or coastal garden; good as screening or divisions

**FLOWERS** May to June

**ASPECT** Any, in a sheltered or exposed position; full sun

**SOIL** Any fertile, well-drained soil

**HARDINESS** Fully hardy at temperatures down to -15°C/5°F; needs no winter protection

**DROUGHT TOLERANCE** Poor

**PROBLEMS** Leaf miners; honey fungus, powdery mildew and silver leaf

**CARE** Cut out dead, diseased or damaged material in late winter or early spring

**PROPAGATION** Sow ripe seed (pre-soaked in hot water for 48 hours) in pots in a cold frame

## *Lathyrus odoratus* 'America' ▢
### Annual sweet pea

⬆ 2m/6ft ⬌ 30cm/12in                    **EASY**

These annual, tendrilled climbers, originally from Sicily, are renowned for their abundant, delicate, fragrant flowers. This variety has oval, pastel green leaves and wiry, grasping stems with fine curly tendrils. Sweetly scented white flowers (up to 5cm/2in long), with pinky red streaking marbled across the frilled-edged petals, are held on straight, slim, smooth sage green stems. Winged pale green pea pods follow the flowers. Other favourites are *L.o.* 'Cupani', with indigo and fuchsia flowers, and *L.o.* 'Black Knight', with velvet black flowers.

> **BEST USES** Excellent for climbing over low walls, trellis and obelisks; great in containers; ideal for growing with climbing and shrub roses

**FLOWERS** July to October

**ASPECT** South or west facing, in a sheltered position with protection from cold winds; full sun to partial shade

**SOIL** Any fertile, humus-rich, well-drained soil

**HARDINESS** Fully hardy at temperatures down to -15°C/5°F; needs no winter protection

**DROUGHT TOLERANCE** Poor

**PROBLEMS** None

**CARE** Pinch out side shoots once seedlings are a few inches high; pick flowers often

**PROPAGATION** Sow pre-soaked seed in pots in a cold frame in early spring or autumn; or sow in final flowering positions in early spring

## *Lilium* 'Casa Blanca' 🎖
Lily

⬆ 1–1.2m/3–4ft ⬌ 50cm/20in      **EASY**

Lilies are bulbous perennials from a wide variety of habitats across Europe, Asia and the USA. This strong-growing variety of Japanese origin has tall, smooth, sturdy mid-green stems with narrow, lance-shaped, fresh green, slightly glossy foliage generously arranged up the stems. Flower buds on branching stems open to reveal large, highly perfumed, trumpet-shaped snow white flowers (up to 30cm/12in across) with petals that curve slightly backwards and distinctive, pollen-dusty cinnamon brown anthers. *L*. 'Star Gazer' is similar, with red and darker freckled scented blooms.

**BEST USES** Perfect for both the cottage garden and formal flower border; excellent as cut flowers

**FLOWERS** July to August
**ASPECT** Any, in a sheltered or exposed position; full sun to partial shade
**SOIL** Any fertile, moist, well-drained soil
**HARDINESS** Fully hardy at temperatures down to -15°C/5°F; needs no winter protection
**DROUGHT TOLERANCE** Poor
**PROBLEMS** Aphids, scarlet lily beetle, slugs and snails; rabbits; *Botrytis* (grey mould)
**CARE** Plant bulbs 20cm/8in deep in autumn; plants may need staking; deadhead spent flowers; cut to ground level in autumn
**PROPAGATION** Division in early spring or autumn

## *Lomatia myricoides*

⬆ 3m/10ft ⬌ 2.5m/8ft      **EASY**

This bushy, upright, evergreen woodland shrub from Australia rarely reaches more than 3m/10ft in height, so is ideal for the small, sunny garden. Some say it's architectural, whereas I think it has a droopy, sprawly gait, but it is charming none the less. It has upright, green-tan stems with long, narrow, tapering, notched leathery dark green leaves (about 20cm/8in long) and pale green stems, tinged red-brown, bearing clusters of spidery, curving, creamy white, exotic, highly fragrant flowers in mid-summer that are madly attractive to pollinating insects. Given a warm south or west-facing wall, it should come through mild winters in colder areas.

**BEST USES** Ideal for both exotic and cottage gardens; perfect as scented screening; good in containers in sheltered city courtyards and patios

**FLOWERS** July
**ASPECT** South, west or east facing, in a sheltered position; full sun to partial shade
**SOIL** Any fertile, moist, well-drained soil
**HARDINESS** Fully hardy/borderline at temperatures down to -15°C/5°F; may need winter protection in colder areas
**DROUGHT TOLERANCE** Poor
**PROBLEMS** None
**CARE** Minimal pruning; cut out dead, diseased or damaged growth in winter or early spring
**PROPAGATION** Softwood cuttings in early summer; semi-ripe cuttings in midsummer

## Nicotiana sylvestris
### Tobacco plant

⬆ 1.5m/5ft ⬌ 60cm/24in      **EASY**

Tobacco plants have a diverse range of origins, from Australia to North and South America, and are a group of (largely) tender plants that include annuals, perennials and shrubs. This tall, sturdy, short-lived perennial (or half-hardy annual) has large, upright, broad oval apple green leaves (about 35cm/14in long) and tall, sturdy, reasonably self-supporting stems, each topped with branching heads of pendulous, long-necked, tubular, exotically fragrant white flowers. The flowers and scent are shy in full sun and are coaxed out as dusk approaches. The compact Domino and Havana series come in a wide range of colours: pinks, reds, salmons and whites.

**BEST USES** Perfect for filling gaps in borders; gorgeous among ornamental grasses; compact varieties thrive in pots and hanging baskets

**FLOWERS** July to September

**ASPECT** South, west or east facing, in a sheltered position; full sun to partial shade

**SOIL** Any fertile, moist, well-drained soil

**HARDINESS** Half hardy at temperatures down to 0°C/32°F; needs winter protection

**DROUGHT TOLERANCE** Poor

**PROBLEMS** Aphids, leafhoppers, slugs and snails; *Botrytis* (grey mould)

**CARE** Water regularly; overwinter in mild areas with a dry mulch and/or fleece

**PROPAGATION** Sow seed in early spring in a frost-free greenhouse

## Perovskia 'Blue Spire'
### Russian sage

⬆ 1.2m/4ft ⬌ 90cm/3ft      **EASY**

This upright sub-shrub from Asia comes into its own mist of pastel glory in late summer to early autumn. It is a tall, upright, woody-based plant with slender, brittle, branched stems and small-leaved, dissected, grey-green aromatic foliage. Hazy spires of tiny tubular lavender-blue flowers are studded along the flower stems. It grows rapidly from unlikely-looking low bare stems up to its full height by the end of the season, but won't tolerate any sort of waterlogging.

**BEST USES** Adds stately, gauzy elegance to the late-summer border or Mediterranean or gravel garden; combines well with grasses or prairie plantings; good in coastal gardens; thrives on chalky soil

**FLOWERS** August to September

**ASPECT** South, west or east facing, in a sheltered or exposed position; full sun

**SOIL** Any fertile to poor, well-drained soil

**HARDINESS** Fully hardy at temperatures down to -15°C/5°F; needs no winter protection

**DROUGHT TOLERANCE** Excellent, once established

**PROBLEMS** None

**CARE** Cut back hard to a low, woody framework, a little above ground level, as the new buds start to unfurl in late spring (be careful not to cut into the new growth)

**PROPAGATION** Semi-ripe cuttings in summer

## *Rosa* Ginger Syllabub

⬆ 3m/10ft ⬌ 2.5m/8ft                    **EASY**

This energetic, elegantly arching climbing rose defies you not to take a hefty lungful of its lingering heady fragrance. It has glossy mid-green, pointed oval leaves and gorgeous cupped, crumpled, double pale amber-peach flowers (up to 10cm/4in across) that bloom through summer. Other fragrant climbing roses include the pale icing pink *R*. 'New Dawn' ♉ (2.5m/8ft × 3m/10ft), flowering July to September, and the orange-scented, semi-double faded purple clusters of *R*. 'Veilchenblau' ♉ (rambler 4m/13ft height and spread), flowering June to July.

**BEST USES** Grow against a large sunny wall or fence, or through a large shrub or old apple tree

**FLOWERS** June to October

**ASPECT** Any, in a sheltered position; full sun

**SOIL** Any fertile, humus-rich, moist, well-drained soil

**HARDINESS** Fully hardy at temperatures down to -15°C/5°F; needs no winter protection

**DROUGHT TOLERANCE** Excellent, once established

**PROBLEMS** Aphids, caterpillars, leafhoppers and scale insects; blackspot, downy and powdery mildew, honey fungus, rose ball, rose soil sickness and rust

**CARE** Mulch with organic matter in late winter or early spring; deadhead spent blooms (where practical); for pruning, see pages 36–7

**PROPAGATION** Hardwood cuttings in autumn

## *Rosa* 'Ispahan' ♉

⬆ 1.5m/5ft ⬌ 1.2m/4ft                    **EASY**

The perfume of this lovely Damask rose is widely acknowledged as being unsurpassed by all the modern hybrids and old roses put together. A fast-growing shrub rose with an upright, open, free-flowering habit and small sage green leaves, it bears stunning, double, rich pink flowers (about 8cm/3in across) on strong stems. Wet or windy weather will spoil the flowers – and there is only one coveted flush – but it is an outstanding rose.

**BEST USES** Ideal for trellis, arbours or low garden walls; excellent in the cottage or formal garden; grows well in containers; deer proof

**FLOWERS** June

**ASPECT** Any, in a sheltered position; full sun to partial shade (flowering will be reduced in shade)

**SOIL** Any fertile, humus-rich, moist, well-drained soil

**HARDINESS** Fully hardy at temperatures down to -15°C/5°F; needs no winter protection

**DROUGHT TOLERANCE** Excellent, once established

**PROBLEMS** Aphids, caterpillars, leafhoppers and scale insects; blackspot, downy and powdery mildew, honey fungus, rose ball, rose soil sickness and rust

**CARE** Mulch with organic matter in late winter or early spring; deadhead spent blooms (where practical); for pruning, see pages 36–7

**PROPAGATION** Hardwood cuttings in autumn

## Rosa 'Guinée'

↑ 2m/6ft ⬌ 5m/16ft         **EASY**

If you favour an extravagant, opulent rose, look no further. This bushy, climbing Hybrid Tea rose has somewhat stiff stems (so tie them in early as they get less pliable with age) and fresh green polished leaves which show off the dramatic, double, dark blood red blooms (up to 8cm/3in across) to full advantage. It has good disease resistance and is one of the darkest red roses on offer.

**BEST USES** Good for formal or cottage gardens; perfect against pillars or trellis, or in pots on a sunny patio or roof terrace; excellent as cut flowers

**FLOWERS** June to July

**ASPECT** South, west or east facing, in a sheltered position; full sun

**SOIL** Any fertile, humus-rich, moist, well-drained soil

**HARDINESS** Fully hardy at temperatures down to -15°C/5°F; needs no winter protection

**DROUGHT TOLERANCE** Excellent, once established

**PROBLEMS** Aphids, caterpillars, leafhoppers and scale insects; blackspot, downy and powdery mildew, honey fungus, rose ball, rose soil sickness and rust

**CARE** Mulch with organic matter in late winter or early spring; deadhead spent blooms; cut out dead, diseased, damaged or weak shoots; for pruning, see pages 36–7

**PROPAGATION** Hardwood cuttings in autumn

## Sambucus nigra 'Gerda' 🎖

(formerly *S.n.* f. *porphyrophylla* 'Black Beauty') Elder

↑ 3m/10ft ⬌ 3m/10ft         **EASY**

Elders originate from as far afield as Europe, Asia and Africa. The common elder is pretty enough, but this cracking variety really stands out from the crowd. An upright, loose shrub, it has claret-green stems and very appealing oval, delicately dissected, fringe-edged leaves of charcoal-burgundy that look good from unfurling in early spring all the way through to autumn. In early summer, generous clusters of deep red buds open to foamy panicles of lemony-fragrant pale pink flowers, wildly attractive to insects. In late summer, it bears dangling bunches of black-purple berries that are loved by birds.

**BEST USES** Enjoys sheltered woodland; good for a wildlife garden; perfect for a hot-coloured planting scheme; excellent for coastal gardens

**FLOWERS** June

**ASPECT** Any, in a sheltered or exposed position; full sun to partial shade

**SOIL** Any fertile, moist, humus-rich, well-drained soil

**HARDINESS** Fully hardy at temperatures down to -15°C/5°F; needs no winter protection

**DROUGHT TOLERANCE** Poor

**PROBLEMS** Aphids (blackfly)

**CARE** For the best foliage effect, cut back to ground level in early spring

**PROPAGATION** Hardwood cuttings in winter

## Brugmansia x candida 'Grand Marnier' 🎖 Angels' trumpets

⬆ 5m/16ft ⬌ 1.5–2.5m/5–8ft    **MEDIUM**

Brugmansias (which used to be known as daturas) are tender, upright, evergreen shrubs from the USA and South America. They have an open, goblet-like habit, with outward-stretching branches clothed in large, oval, slightly coarse mid-green leaves. The extravagant, wavy-edged flowers form large, pendent pale apricot trumpets (up to 30cm/12in long) that diffuse a strong sweet perfume as night falls. Growth is rapid once they are settled. All parts are toxic and hallucinogenic.

**BEST USES** Architectural plants for a warm city patio; grow in pots to fill gaps in the summer border

**FLOWERS** July to September

**ASPECT** South or west facing, in a sheltered position; full sun

**SOIL** Any fertile, well-drained soil

**HARDINESS** Frost tender at temperatures below 5°C/41°F; in cold regions, grow in a frost-free greenhouse or conservatory and move outside in summer

**DROUGHT TOLERANCE** Poor

**PROBLEMS** Aphids and red spider mite (indoors)

**CARE** Deadhead spent flowers regularly; cut flowered shoots to within 2–3 buds of the base in early spring, removing dead or diseased material

**PROPAGATION** Semi-ripe cuttings with bottom heat in summer

**GREENFINGER TIP** *With protection, these often come through the winter in southern city gardens*

## Clematis rehderiana 🎖 Nodding virgin's bower

⬆ 7m/22ft ⬌ 2.5m/8ft    **EASY**

This fast-growing late-flowering clematis of Chinese origin is a great climber to introduce into the late-summer and autumn garden, with its mid-green serrated-edged leaves providing an attractive backdrop for the dainty, pale creamy-tinted yellow bells of nodding flowers (about 2cm/¾in long), suspended from slender, pale limey stems. The flowers, which resemble little Chinese paper lanterns, are abundantly produced in clusters and smell as sweetly as primrose, with appealing pronounced yellow anthers.

**BEST USES** Grow through trees or shrubs that are past their flowering best; perfect for clothing walls, sheds or unsightly outbuildings

**FLOWERS** July to October

**ASPECT** Any, in a sheltered or exposed position; full sun to partial shade

**SOIL** Any fertile, moist, well-drained soil

**HARDINESS** Fully hardy at temperatures down to -15°C/5°F; needs no winter protection

**DROUGHT TOLERANCE** Poor

**PROBLEMS** Earwigs; clematis wilt

**CARE** Cut back the previous year's growth to a healthy pair of buds, about 15–20cm/6–8in above ground level, before new growth starts in early spring

**PROPAGATION** Semi-ripe cuttings in late summer

**GREENFINGER TIP** *Plant clematis deeper than the pot, with a couple of buds buried below ground level as insurance against clematis wilt*

## *Clerodendrum trichotomum*
### Glory flower

⬆ 5–6m/16–20ft ⬌ 5–6m/16–20ft          **EASY**

This upright, bushy, mounded, deciduous shrub of Chinese origin has outward-reaching branches and large, heart-shaped, mid-green leaves (up to 20cm/8in long) with marked veining. These smell unpleasant if bruised, but the hanging clusters of tiny, tubular, star-shaped white flowers smell as sweet as lemony honeysuckle. I love this plant best in autumn, when inedible bright turquoise berries framed by striking starry scarlet calyces dangle vividly from the branches against the yellowing leaves. *C. bungei* is more compact (2m/6ft height and spread) and has domed clusters of fragrant pink tubular flowers.

**BEST USES** An easy plant for informal or cottage gardens; thrives in pots in a sunny courtyard

**FLOWERS** August to October

**ASPECT** South or west facing, in a sheltered position; full sun

**SOIL** Any fertile, humus-rich, moist, well-drained soil

**HARDINESS** Fully hardy at temperatures down to -15°C/5°F; needs no winter protection

**DROUGHT TOLERANCE** Poor

**PROBLEMS** None

**CARE** Cut out dead, diseased or damaged matter in winter; cut unruly or damaged plants to ground level in winter (new shoots will grow from the base); dig out unwanted suckering shoots

**PROPAGATION** Semi-ripe cuttings in a heated propagator in summer; root cuttings in winter

## *Cordyline australis* ☙
### Cabbage palm

⬆ 3–10m/10–32ft ⬌ 1–4m/3–13ft          **EASY**

Cabbage palms, originally from New Zealand, are now epidemic in containers or stony starved beds in cities across the UK. They are architectural trees with rough, pale tan trunks and this popular variety has slightly arching, tough, mid-green sword-like leaves (up to 90cm/3ft long) festooning from the top of the trunk to form a spiky ball. Mature trees bear tiny off-white flowers in summer, massed together in pendulous panicles. These are incredibly sweetly scented, and even the roots have a gingery tang. Other varieties include *C.a.* 'Torbay Dazzler' ☙ (green and cream-striped foliage) and *C.a.* 'Albertii' ☙ (green leaves with pink midribs).

**BEST USES** An architectural plant for coastal, Mediterranean or exotic gardens; great in pots

**FLOWERS** August to September

**ASPECT** South or west facing, in a sheltered position; full sun to partial shade

**SOIL** Any fertile, moist, well-drained soil

**HARDINESS** Frost hardy at temperatures down to -5°C/23°F; needs winter protection

**DROUGHT TOLERANCE** Excellent, once established

**PROBLEMS** None

**CARE** Pull browned dead leaves from the trunk

**PROPAGATION** Peel rooted suckers from the base in spring and pot up

## *Cytisus battandieri* 🏅
Pineapple broom

⬆ 5m/16ft ↔ 5m/16ft      **EASY**

This is an energetic, upright, deciduous shrub that looks and smells as if it comes from somewhere warm and colourful, and it does – Morocco. Allow plenty of room when planting, as it makes a large, loosely spreading plant with tactile, silky soft, oval, pastel green leaves. Come summer, it is smothered with pineapple-scented pea-like sun gold flowers in erect spired clusters (about 15cm/6in long) and is abuzz with a loyal following of humming bees. Grow it in a sun-blasted hot spot or train it against a warm wall to see it at its best.

**BEST USES** A great focal point in the Mediterranean garden; much loved by pollinating insects; does well in coastal gardens

**FLOWERS** June to July

**ASPECT** South or west facing, in a sheltered position with protection from cold winds; full sun

**SOIL** Any fertile, well-drained soil

**HARDINESS** Frost hardy at temperatures down to -5°/23°F; needs winter protection

**DROUGHT TOLERANCE** Excellent, once established

**PROBLEMS** Gall mites

**CARE** Minimal pruning: cut out dead, diseased or damaged wood in winter or early spring

**PROPAGATION** Semi-ripe cuttings in summer

## *Genista aetnensis* 🏅
Mount Etna broom

⬆ 8m/26ft ↔ 8m/26ft      **EASY**

This deciduous Italian shrub or small tree has a mounded, weeping habit with elegant branches draped in tiny, linear, deep green leaves. The free-flowering, sweetly fragrant golden yellow pea-like flowers are massed along the pendent shoots in summer. If you live in a city in the south, you should have no trouble getting this through a cold winter, but it can be short-lived on heavy clay soils in colder areas.

**BEST USES** Excellent for coastal gardens or exposed windy sites; a handsome addition to the gravel and Mediterranean garden

**FLOWERS** June to July

**ASPECT** Any, in a sheltered or exposed position; full sun

**SOIL** Any fertile, well-drained soil

**HARDINESS** Frost hardy at temperatures down to -5°C/23°F; needs winter protection

**DROUGHT TOLERANCE** Excellent, once established

**PROBLEMS** Rabbits

**CARE** In winter, cut out dead, diseased or damaged wood

**PROPAGATION** Sow seed in pots in a cold frame in autumn or spring; semi-ripe cuttings in summer

## Itea ilicifolia
Holly-leaf sweetspire

⬆ 5m/16ft ⬌ 3m/10ft          **MEDIUM**

This architectural, spreading evergreen shrub
from China is slow-growing, with weeping stems
that are densely clothed in highly polished, holly-
like prickly-edged dark green leaves (10cm/4in
long). From summer through to early autumn, it
produces tiny, vanilla-scented greenish flowers
(6mm/¼in across), which are unremarkable in
themselves but form elegant, catkin-like strings
(up to 30cm/12in long), giving the impression
that the whole shrub is draped in tiered silken
tassels. Fantastic as a stand-alone shrub, this is
perhaps even better grown as a wall shrub.

**BEST USES** Excellent for a warm border or wall;
ideal in a large pot on a sunny city patio

**FLOWERS** July to September
**ASPECT** South or west facing, in a sheltered position
with protection from cold winds; full sun to partial
shade
**SOIL** Any fertile, moist, well-drained soil
**HARDINESS** Frost hardy at temperatures down to
-5°C/23°F; needs winter protection
**DROUGHT TOLERANCE** Poor
**PROBLEMS** None
**CARE** Mulch young plants with organic matter in early
spring or autumn; cut out dead, diseased or damaged
wood in spring; trim wall-grown shrubs lightly after
flowering to maintain size and shape
**PROPAGATION** Sow ripe seed immediately in pots in a
cold frame; semi-ripe cuttings in summer in a heated
propagator

## Magnolia grandiflora
Magnolia

⬆ 6–18m/20–60ft ⬌ 15m/50ft          **EASY**

An elegant and gracious evergreen tree from the
USA, this has a conical but broad, upright habit
and is often grown as a large wall shrub (it will
reach a height of 6m/20ft in twenty-five years). It
has long, oval, leathery green leaves, with suede-
like undersides, held on strong upward-reaching
branches. The upright, conical flower buds start
out beige-green, then whiten, resembling large
ostrich eggs. Each opens to reveal a sumptuous,
bowl-shaped, creamy white waxy flower. The
slightly overlapping cupped petals (up to
25cm/10in across) exude an exquisite, clean
lemon-vanilla fragrance and have raspberry-
streaked bases. The plump, upright stamens
resemble miniature creamy yellow pineapples.

**BEST USES** As a focal point in a large flowerbed or
lawn; as a wall shrub against a large warm wall

**FLOWERS** August to September
**ASPECT** South, west or east facing, in a sheltered
position; full sun
**SOIL** Any fertile, humus-rich, well-drained soil
**HARDINESS** Frost hardy at temperatures down to
-5°C/23°F; needs winter protection; mature trees can
survive temperature dips if sheltered
**DROUGHT TOLERANCE** Good, once established
**PROBLEMS** Scale insects and coral spot
**CARE** In spring, cut out dead, diseased or damaged
material
**PROPAGATION** Sow ripe seed in pots in a cold frame;
buy a named variety from a good nursery

## *Olearia macrodonta* ⚭
### Daisy bush

⬆ 6m/20ft ⬌ 5m/16ft                    **EASY**

This evergreen New Zealander is easy to grow as a small tree or shrub, and has two scents on offer. It has an upright, rounded habit with appealing peeling papery bark and oval, prickly, slightly wavy-edged, dark green musk-scented leaves with silver white undersides, which are attractive in themselves. The honey-scented, white, daisy-like flowers (about 15cm/6in across) appear in clusters aplenty in early summer, attracting bees from the moment flowering starts. Buff-coloured seed heads follow the flowers.

> **BEST USES** Ideal for hedging in seaside gardens; good ground cover for awkward slopes or banks; excellent in pots on sunny patios

**FLOWERS** June
**ASPECT** South, west or east facing, in a sheltered position; full sun
**SOIL** Any fertile, well-drained soil
**HARDINESS** Fully hardy/borderline at temperatures down to -15°C/5°F; may need winter protection in colder areas
**DROUGHT TOLERANCE** Excellent, once established
**PROBLEMS** None
**CARE** Trim lightly after flowering
**PROPAGATION** Semi-ripe cuttings in summer

••••••••••••••••••••••••••••••••••••••••••

**GREENFINGER TIP** *My first outing with this plant, many years ago, was growing it as a hedge in chilly East Anglia; I pruned it in winter and killed the lot. A lesson learnt*

## *Passiflora caerulea* ⚭
### Passionflower

⬆ 10m/32ft ⬌ 10m/32ft                  **EASY**

This evergreen, twining climber comes from Central and South America and doesn't look as if it will be able to cope with a chilly climate, but its exoticism belies an altogether hardier nature. It has attractive lobed, deep green leaves (up to 10cm/4in long) and fragrant, beguilingly graphic white flowers, with distinctive purple-blue filaments circling the pale lime green centres. The flowers are followed by large, egg-shaped vibrant orange fruits, which are edible (though somewhat tasteless). It grows rapidly once it has settled in, so allow plenty of space. *P.c.* 'Constance Elliott' has white flowers with damson-coloured stamens.

> **BEST USES** Ideal on a sunny wall or over a large arbour; unbeatable for covering an ugly fence

**FLOWERS** July to September
**ASPECT** South or west facing, in a sheltered position; full sun to partial shade
**SOIL** Any fertile, moist, well-drained soil
**HARDINESS** Frost hardy at temperatures down to -5°C/23°F; needs winter protection
**DROUGHT TOLERANCE** Excellent, once established
**PROBLEMS** None
**CARE** Trim lightly after flowering, cutting back flowering shoots to within 2–3 buds of the main framework; cut out any dead, diseased or damaged wood as you go
**PROPAGATION** Semi-ripe cuttings in summer; layering in spring

## Rosa 'Bobbie James' 🎖

⬆ 10m/32ft ↔ 6m/20ft                    **EASY**

There are few ramblers to compete with this exuberantly flowering, rampant, rambling rose. It has attractive small, pointed, glossy deep green leaves and, come summer, bears extravagant numbers of small, but sweetly and deeply perfumed, creamy white flowers in trusses about 5cm/2in across. Don't be put off by the blossoms' size: they are profuse in flower and fragrance.

**BEST USES** Ideal for growing on large walls or outbuildings; grow through large, evergreen trees

**FLOWERS** June to July

**ASPECT** Any, in a sheltered position; full sun

**SOIL** Any fertile, humus-rich, moist, well-drained soil

**HARDINESS** Fully hardy at temperatures down to -15°C/5°F; needs no winter protection

**DROUGHT TOLERANCE** Excellent, once established

**PROBLEMS** Aphids, caterpillars, leafhoppers and scale insects; blackspot, downy and powdery mildew, honey fungus, rose ball, rose soil sickness and rust

**CARE** Mulch with organic matter in late winter or early spring; deadhead spent blooms (where practical); for pruning, see pages 36–7

**PROPAGATION** Hardwood cuttings in autumn

**GREENFINGER TIP** *Within three years, deadheading will only be practical with scaffolding*

## Trachelospermum jasminoides 🎖
### Confederate jasmine

⬆ 4.5m/15ft ↔ 3m/10ft                    **MEDIUM**

The deliciously sweet waft from this vigorous, woody, evergreen twining climber from Asia can be scented long before the plant comes into view. And then, on encounter, it doesn't disappoint: it looks as heavenly as it smells, with elegant, smallish, lance-shaped, polished dark green leaves (about 8cm/3in wide) and an abundance of very fragrant, star-shaped, pure white flowers that attract every nectar collector for miles around. It is fairly restrained in its growth habit in the UK, so expect a plant of about 2m/6ft height and spread within five years.

**BEST USES** Adds romance to a sunny patio or courtyard; ideal at the base of a sheltered trellis or sunny wall; grows well in containers on a sunny, sheltered city balcony

**FLOWERS** July to August

**ASPECT** South or west facing, in a sheltered position; full sun to partial shade

**SOIL** Any fertile, moist, well-drained soil

**HARDINESS** Frost hardy at temperatures down to -5°C/23°F; needs winter protection; protect with fleece in cold areas

**DROUGHT TOLERANCE** Poor

**PROBLEMS** Mealybugs and red spider mite (indoors); none outdoors

**CARE** Trim lightly to maintain size and shape in early spring

**PROPAGATION** Semi-ripe cuttings with bottom heat in summer; layering in autumn

# AUTUMN

Autumn is a lean time for floral fragrances. Most pollinating insects have completed their year's work and are dozy, thinking about a long winter's nap, or slowly dying off, and plants aren't going to waste too much effort on perfume production if they can't attract pollinators. Many plants are also retiring into dormancy, enabling them to rebuild their reserves for next year's encore. However, there are several glorious floral scents that still persist and autumn provides its own mellow aromas: the smell of the bonfire; the subtle aroma of the garden after the rain; the scent of woodsmoke drifting across the fields and the sharp icy bite of a frosty autumn morning.

*Amaryllis belladonna*

⬆ 60cm/24in ⬌ 10cm/4in          MEDIUM

This spectacular South African bulbous perennial needs to be kept frost free to thrive. The large bulb has handsome dark green, fleshy, strappy leaves (up to 50cm/20in long) which shoot up after the flowers have appeared, lasting through the winter. The tall, sturdy purple stems are topped with up to six, sharply fragrant, overtly flared pale pink trumpets (up to 10cm/4in long), suffused yellow at the base, with prominent, creamy flushed rose, spidery stamens. *A.b.* 'Johannesburg' is paler rosy pink.

**BEST USES** Grow under a south-facing wall for maximum heat in summer; in containers on a sunny patio, or in a greenhouse or conservatory

**FLOWERS** September to November
**ASPECT** South, west or east facing, in a sheltered position; full sun
**SOIL** Any fertile, moist, well-drained soil
**HARDINESS** Frost hardy at temperatures down to -5°C/23°F; needs winter protection
**DROUGHT TOLERANCE** Excellent, once established
**PROBLEMS** Aphids, narcissus bulb fly, narcissus eelworms, slugs and snails; red spider mite (indoors)
**CARE** Plant bulbs in late summer or spring, with their tops just below the soil surface; mulch with straw in frost-prone areas
**PROPAGATION** Buy fresh bulbs in mid-summer; remove young offsets in spring

## *Chrysanthemum* 'Carmine Blush'

⬆ 60cm/24in ⬅➡ 75cm/30in          **EASY**

Chrysanthemums originate from Asia to Russia and many are best suited to indoor cultivation. However, the hardy outdoor varieties are enjoying a resurgence, and often have good mildew resistance nowadays. This reliable, clump-forming, bushy, woody-based perennial has coarse-toothed deep green leaves, making dense, rounded, upright plants. The branched stems hold sprays of lightly scented rayed-petalled flowers (like large daisies) which are vibrant pink with distinct yellow centres.

**BEST USES** Ideal for adding colour to formal or informal late-autumn borders; does well in pots

**FLOWERS** October to December

**ASPECT** South or west facing, in a sheltered position; full sun

**SOIL** Any fertile, humus-rich, well-drained soil; prefers slight acidity

**HARDINESS** Fully hardy at temperatures down to -15°C/5°F; needs no winter protection

**DROUGHT TOLERANCE** Poor

**PROBLEMS** Aphids, capsid bugs, earwigs and eelworms; *Botrytis* (grey mould), powdery mildew and rust

**CARE** Cut back to woody growth in early spring; pinch out the growing tips when they are about 20cm/8in tall, to encourage flowering shoots; may need staking (this variety is fairly self-supporting)

**PROPAGATION** Division in spring; basal cuttings in late winter, to overwinter in a greenhouse

## *Cyclamen hederifolium* 🎖
### Sowbread

⬆ 10–13cm/4–5in ⬅➡ 15cm/6in          **EASY**

This tuberous Mediterranean perennial has ivy-like, heart-shaped green leaves, marbled with cream and splashed deeper green in the centre. It makes rounded clumps of glossy, long-lasting foliage that are an appealing foil for the dainty, upright, winged flowers (about 2.5cm/1in long), like butterflies at rest, which are rich pink, flushed plum at the base, and carried on smooth, slender, short, reddish stems from mid to late autumn. Some of the flowers are sweetly scented, some not – don't ask me why. They are likely to appear shortly before the leaves.

**BEST USES** Thrives under trees or by hedges, where little else will grow; looks good at the front of a border or in any gloomy city garden or patio

**FLOWERS** October to January

**ASPECT** Any, in a sheltered position; full sun to partial shade

**SOIL** Any humus-rich, moist, well-drained soil; dislikes sitting in wet

**HARDINESS** Fully hardy at temperatures down to -15°C/5°F; needs no winter protection

**DROUGHT TOLERANCE** Poor

**PROBLEMS** Vine weevil; mice and squirrels

**CARE** Plant tubers 5cm/2in deep in any soil, enriched with leafmould

**PROPAGATION** Self-seeds reasonably well; sow ripe seed immediately in pots in a cold frame; division in spring

## *Chaenomeles* × *superba* 'Pink Lady' 🎖
Japanese quince

⬆ 1.5m/5ft ⬌ 2m/6ft                    EASY

Quinces are thorny, spreading, deciduous shrubs from China and Japan, and offer dainty elegance in the winter garden. Although the flowers are not fragrant, they do have remarkable scented autumn fruits. This thornless variety has small, rounded, glossy leaves (about 6cm/2½in long) and bears rich pink buds on bare stems, before the leaves appear. They open to deep rose pink, shallow-bowled flowers with striking golden stamens (about 5cm/2in across). Then come the small pale green fruits, the size of crab apples, which ripen to yellow in autumn and have a heavenly fragrance.

**BEST USES** Perfect as a wall-trained shrub or for growing against fences and trellis

**FLOWERS** March to May (fruit in September)

**ASPECT** Any, in a sheltered or exposed position; full sun to partial shade

**SOIL** Any fertile, moist, well-drained soil

**HARDINESS** Fully hardy at temperatures down to -15°C/5°F; needs no winter protection

**DROUGHT TOLERANCE** Excellent, once established

**PROBLEMS** Aphids and scale insects; fireblight

**CARE** After flowering, cut side shoots back to six leaves; cut out any dead, diseased or damaged material as you go

**PROPAGATION** Semi-ripe cuttings in summer; hardwood cuttings in winter; layering in winter

## *Elaeagnus* × *ebbingei* 'Gilt Edge' 🎖

⬆ 3m/10ft ⬌ 3m/10ft                    EASY

A reliable, fast-growing evergreen shrub from Japan, this has tawny bark and slightly felty stems, and soon makes a dense, bushy plant. The pointed oval, shiny, deep green-centred leaves are edged in creamy yellow, with the undersides upholstered in a silver fur. The dangling clusters of small, tubular, creamy white flowers are not showy, but are as sweetly fragrant as they come. If you catch a delicious whiff that you can't identify on an autumn day, the chances are this is the source. Brown berries that deepen to red follow after the flowers have faded.

**BEST USES** Ideal as a specimen in a mixed border or shrubbery; good ground cover on banks; great for hedges and screens; good for seaside gardens

**FLOWERS** October to November

**ASPECT** Any, in a sheltered or exposed position; full sun to partial shade (but leaf variegation is more pronounced in full sun)

**SOIL** Any fertile, moist, well-drained soil

**HARDINESS** Fully hardy at temperatures down to -15°C/5°F; needs no winter protection

**DROUGHT TOLERANCE** Excellent, once established

**PROBLEMS** Coral spot

**CARE** Trim in late summer; cut out any shoots with solid green leaves as they appear, to keep the leaf variegation

**PROPAGATION** Semi-ripe cuttings in summer

## *Hamamelis virginiana*
### Virginian witch hazel

⬆ 4m/13ft ⬌ 4m/13ft                                    EASY

We are used to seeing the distinctive, spidery flowers of witch hazel in winter, so this variety, offering both fragrance and flower in autumn, is invaluable. An upright, deciduous shrub from North America, it has attractive, rounded, mid-green leaves (about 15cm/6in long) that yellow as autumn approaches. As the leaves begin to fall, clusters of small, sweetly scented, spidery yellow flowers appear on the nearly bare branches. It is perhaps not the most beautiful of the witch hazels, but well worth growing for autumn interest.

**BEST USES** Perfect for a woodland garden or mixed shrub border; enlivens a dull corner of the garden in dappled shade

**FLOWERS** October

**ASPECT** Any, in a sheltered position; full sun to partial shade

**SOIL** Any fertile, moist, well-drained, neutral to slightly acid soil

**HARDINESS** Fully hardy at temperatures down to -15°C/5°F; needs no winter protection

**DROUGHT TOLERANCE** Poor

**PROBLEMS** Coral spot and honey fungus

**CARE** Cut out any dead, diseased or damaged material in late winter

**PROPAGATION** Sow seed in pots in a cold frame in spring and keep seedlings frost free

## *Viburnum farreri* ⚇

⬆ 3m/10ft ⬌ 3m/10ft                                    EASY

Many of the deciduous and evergreen viburnums offer both fragrance and flowering interest in the autumn and winter months, making them indispensable in the garden. This charming and graceful deciduous shrub from China has handsome oval, bronze baby leaves, ageing to dark green before colouring in autumn to muted burgundy shades. From autumn the bare branches are studded with clusters of tiny, tubular, pinky white blossoms (about 1cm/½in long), borne in sufficient profusion to create a sweetly fragrant impact on a dull day. Small rounded, pillar-box red berries follow the flowers, encouraging wildlife into the garden.

**BEST USES** Makes elegant hedging or screening; ideal in a dappled shady border or a woodland garden

**FLOWERS** November to February

**ASPECT** Any, in a sheltered or exposed position; full sun to partial shade

**SOIL** Any fertile, moist, well-drained soil

**HARDINESS** Fully hardy at temperatures down to -15°C/5°F; needs no winter protection

**DROUGHT TOLERANCE** Excellent, once established

**PROBLEMS** Aphids and viburnum beetle

**CARE** Trim lightly after flowering; to renovate older bushes, prune hard after flowering

**PROPAGATION** Greenwood cuttings in summer

## *Arbutus unedo* 🏅
### Strawberry tree

⬆ 8m/26ft ↔ 8m/26ft **EASY**

This slow-growing evergreen tree (or very large shrub) from south-eastern Europe has a rounded, spreading shape with rough, conker brown, peeling bark and oval pointed, polished mid-green leaves, held on green stems that are pink-tinged when young. The foliage is a perfect backdrop to the clusters of honey-scented creamy white flowers, often with a pink flush, which dangle cheerfully in autumn, alongside the hanging bunches of strawberry-like fruits (about 2cm/¾in across). These are edible, but bland, and take nearly a year to ripen, so fruits and flower are often present simultaneously. Birds love the fruit. This needs plenty of room. *A.u.* 'Compacta' (3.5m/12ft tall) is a better choice for a small garden.

**BEST USES** Does well in seaside and woodland gardens; ideal as a specimen in a formal lawn

**FLOWERS** September to November

**ASPECT** Any, in a sheltered or exposed position; full sun to partial shade

**SOIL** Any fertile, moist, well-drained, acid soil

**HARDINESS** Fully hardy at temperatures down to -15°C/5°F; needs no winter protection

**DROUGHT TOLERANCE** Good, once established

**PROBLEMS** Aphids; leaf spot

**CARE** Cut out dead, diseased or damaged wood in late winter or early spring

**PROPAGATION** Semi-ripe cuttings in late summer

## *Camellia sasanqua* 'Crimson King' 🏅

⬆ 6m/20ft ↔ 3m/10ft **EASY**

Camellias are famed for their handsome evergreen foliage and showy flowers, usually appearing in spring, and many of the newer Japanese species are fragrant too. This elegant, formal, rounded, spreading shrub from east Asia has broadly elliptical, leathery, glossy dark green leaves, often flushed pinky bronze when young, and in autumn bears large, cupped, single deep crimson flowers with rich golden centres and a sweet, tea-scented fragrance.

**BEST USES** Does well in large pots in city or patio gardens; excellent as architectural interest in large flowerbeds or mixed shrubberies; ideal ground cover in awkward corners or on banks

**FLOWERS** November to February

**ASPECT** Any, in a sheltered position with protection from strong winds; partial to full shade (can take full sun once established)

**SOIL** Any fertile, moist, well-drained, acid soil

**HARDINESS** Fully hardy at temperatures down to -15°C/5°F; needs no winter protection

**DROUGHT TOLERANCE** Poor

**PROBLEMS** Aphids and vine weevil; sooty mould

**CARE** Trim lightly after flowering, cutting out any dead, diseased or damaged material; an older unruly shrub can take hard pruning, to renovate

**PROPAGATION** Semi-ripe cuttings in summer

**GREENFINGER TIP** *Don't plant in an east-facing spot: after frost, the morning sun browns the blooms*

## *Heptacodium miconioides*
### Seven son flower

⬆ 6m/20ft ↔ 2.5–3m/8–10ft     **EASY**

This fairly fast-growing, multi-branched shrub or mounded small tree from China has a lot to offer for all seasons, as well as being easy to grow. The pointed, oval, vein-etched pale green leaves are curved like horns, and tinted burgundy in autumn. Clusters of very dainty, sweetly scented starry white flowers bloom at the tips of the branches from late summer. The flowers drop once the frosts bite, leaving behind rosy calyces that darken to claret; rounded red berries often follow the flowers. In winter it has attractive grey peeling bark and the young branches are flushed red. It must rate 10/10 for year-round interest.

**BEST USES** Good for cottage gardens; excellent as a focal point in a lawn or mixed shrub border; ideal for coastal gardens

**FLOWERS** August to November

**ASPECT** Any, in a sheltered or exposed position; full sun to partial shade

**SOIL** Any fertile, moist, well-drained soil

**HARDINESS** Fully hardy at temperatures down to -15°C/5°F; needs no winter protection

**DROUGHT TOLERANCE** Good, once established

**PROBLEMS** None

**CARE** Cut out dead, diseased or damaged wood in late winter to early spring

**PROPAGATION** Hardwood cuttings in autumn

## *Humulus lupulus* 'Aureus'
### Golden hop

⬆ 6m/20ft ↔ 6m/20ft     **EASY**

This fast-growing, twining, climbing herbaceous perennial originates in areas from Asia to Europe. The coarse, toothed-edged, bright gold leaves (15cm/6in long) glow with the late slanting sun. In July, oval, scaled, cone-like, pale green flowers or hops (about 2cm/¾in long) waft their sun-warmed beery scent, luring butterflies and bees from miles around, before turning buff-coloured in autumn. The plant dies back completely in winter.

**BEST USES** Excellent growing along sunny walls, fences and trellis, over sturdy archways and pergolas, or through large shrubs or trees

**FLOWERS** July to September, but grown mainly for summer foliage and autumn hops

**ASPECT** South, west or east facing, in a sheltered position with protection from cold winds; full sun (in partial shade, leaf colour will be greener and flowering reduced)

**SOIL** Any fertile, humus-rich, well-drained soil, including chalk

**HARDINESS** Fully hardy at temperatures down to -15°C/5°F; needs no winter protection

**DROUGHT TOLERANCE** Good, once established

**PROBLEMS** *Verticillium* wilt

**CARE** Cut back all foliage to ground level in winter or early spring

**PROPAGATION** Softwood cuttings in spring; semi-ripe cuttings in a heated propagator in summer

# WINTER

Most perennials and flowering trees and shrubs are over now and the fragrant flowering glories of the gardening year are but a lingering memory. We tend to think of winter as a time of floral dearth, yet many of the winter-flowering shrubs have much to offer in the perfume department. The choice is nowhere near as wide as in the warmer spring and summer months, but all the more reason to covet those lovely plants that so willingly bring their unique perfumed enchantments into the hostile, chilly, winter landscape, where others fear to tread. Thank heaven for them.

## *Coronilla valentina* subsp. *glauca* 'Citrina' ⚇

⬆ 80cm/32in ⬌ 80cm/32in  **EASY**

Here is a Mediterranean shrub that flowers its head off in winter and spring (and obligingly flowers yet again in summer). It is a rounded, bushy, evergreen shrub, with small, rounded, sage green leaves that make it look like a sun-worshipper better suited to a baking hot summer border. But no! Not this chap. A cold wintry snap is all the encouragement it needs to produce its generous clusters of daffodil-fragranced, pale butter yellow pea-like flowers from November to March and again in summer. Slender pea pods follow the flowers. What more could you ask?

**BEST USES** Unbeatable as ground cover in beds and on slopes; great in pots on a hot sunny patio; an ideal candidate for the Mediterranean or gravel garden

**FLOWERS** November to March; May to July

**ASPECT** South or west facing, in a sheltered position with protection from cold winds; full sun

**SOIL** Any fertile, well-drained soil

**HARDINESS** Frost hardy at temperatures down to -5°C/23°F; needs winter protection

**DROUGHT TOLERANCE** Excellent, once established

**PROBLEMS** None

**CARE** Low maintenance

**PROPAGATION** Sow ripe seed immediately in pots in a cold frame; semi-ripe cuttings in summer

## *Galanthus* 'S. Arnott'
### Snowdrop

⬆ 20cm/8in ⬌ 8cm/3in      **EASY**

Which of us can resist the pure, snowy charms of the snowdrop? These bulbous perennials are found widely from Europe to Asia and have slender, smooth, fresh green stems with smooth, narrow, blade-like green leaves. Each stem is topped with nodding, three-petalled pure white flowers that are sweetly honey-scented. In this appealing variety each inner tepal is marked with a distinct bright green V-shaped banding on the interior. *G. nivalis* 'Viridapice' has pale apple green blotching on the outer petal tips; *G.n.* f. *pleniflorus* 'Flore Pleno' has double white blooms.

**BEST USES** Ideal for naturalising in rough grassy areas; good in pots or in a mixed border

**FLOWERS** February to March
**ASPECT** South, west or east facing, in a sheltered position; full sun to partial shade
**SOIL** Fertile, moist, humus-rich, well-drained soil
**HARDINESS** Fully hardy at temperatures down to -15°C/5°F; needs no winter protection
**DROUGHT TOLERANCE** Poor
**PROBLEMS** Narcissus bulb fly and narcissus eelworms; *Botrytis* (grey mould)
**CARE** Plant bulbs in autumn, 5–8cm/2–3in deep
**PROPAGATION** Division as the leaves are dying back

........................................................

**GREENFINGER TIP** *Snowdrops establish better planted while still growing, known as being 'in the green'; dried bulbs take longer to settle*

## *Iris* 'Harmony' (Reticulata)

⬆ 15cm/6in ⬌ 8cm/3in      **EASY**

Irises are rhizomatous or bulbous perennials native to the northern hemisphere, and are usually deciduous (some are evergreen). They may be tall or short, come in a breathtaking colour range and many are scented. Most flower in spring or summer, but the indispensable Reticulatas bloom from winter to spring. This charming, small, bulbous variety has narrow, upright, bladed grey-green leaves from which emerge slim, smooth stems with single, rich deep blue-mauve perfumed flowers (about 8cm/3in across) with white specking and vivid yellow streaking on their petals. They look as though they have been handpainted – bliss.

**BEST USES** Ideal in a cottage garden; grows well through gravel or in pots

**FLOWERS** February to March
**ASPECT** Any, in a sheltered or exposed position; full sun
**SOIL** Any fertile, moist, well-drained soil
**HARDINESS** Fully hardy at temperatures down to -15°C/5°F; needs no winter protection
**DROUGHT TOLERANCE** Poor
**PROBLEMS** Slugs and snails; ink spot
**CARE** Feed annually with bulb fertiliser when growing
**PROPAGATION** Division in summer to autumn

........................................................

**GREENFINGER TIP** *Some bulbs will die each season, so add a few every year for a lush carpet*

## *Scilla mischtschenkoana* 'Tubergeniana'

⬆ 15cm/6in ⬌ 10cm/4in      **EASY**

The practically unpronounceable name is one heck of a mouthful for this diminutive bulbous perennial from Armenia. Although not as widely known as other winter-flowering bulbs, it certainly offers dainty late-winter cheer among the more popular snowdrops. It has very slender mid-green stems with arching, lance-shaped, bright green leaves (up to 10cm/4in long); each stem is densely packed with clustered, sweetly fragrant star-shaped white flowers, tinted with a faint icy blue glaze.

> **BEST USES** Fantastic in the late-winter and early spring border, or leave to naturalise in rough grass; good in pots, troughs and containers

**FLOWERS** February to March

**ASPECT** Any, in a sheltered or exposed position; full sun to partial shade

**SOIL** Any fertile, humus-rich, moist, well-drained soil

**HARDINESS** Fully hardy at temperatures down to -15°C/5°F; needs no winter protection

**DROUGHT TOLERANCE** Poor

**PROBLEMS** None

**CARE** Plant bulbs in late summer, 8cm/3in deep and up to 8cm/3in apart

**PROPAGATION** Division every four or five years, in late summer

## *Viola odorata*
### English violet

⬆ 20cm/8in ⬌ 30cm/12in      **EASY**

This evergreen perennial from Europe is a classic cottage garden favourite that is sweetly fragrant. It spreads by creeping rhizomes and has heart-shaped, fresh mid-green leaves making rounded, low-growing mounds. Masses of simple, dainty, gappy five-petalled blue or white flowers are produced on short, slender stems, from late winter into early spring. (P.S. In my experience, violets prove a reliable barometer of good character: if ever you meet someone who detests violets, treat them with suspicion . . . )

> **BEST USES** A natural for the cottage or 'blue and white' garden; ideal in pots and containers; makes good ground cover in a woodland garden

**FLOWERS** February to March

**ASPECT** South, west or east facing, in a sheltered position; full sun to partial shade

**SOIL** Any fertile, well-drained soil

**HARDINESS** Fully hardy at temperatures down to -15°C/5°F; needs no winter protection

**DROUGHT TOLERANCE** Poor

**PROBLEMS** Aphids, gall midges, slugs and snails; powdery mildew and rust

**CARE** Prune lightly after flowering

**PROPAGATION** Self-seeds easily; division in spring

## Abeliophyllum distichum
### White forsythia

⬆ 1.5m/5ft ⬌ 1.5m/5ft                    EASY

This Korean native is a somewhat untidy, rounded, deciduous shrub with a lax habit and knobbly, dark brown branches. Before the deep green oval leaves (about 8cm/3in long) emerge, bunched clusters of purple buds open to extremely fragrant, star-shaped creamy white flowers along the bare stems. Winged fruits follow the flowers and the foliage turns claret in autumn.

**BEST USES** Shapes up more neatly as a wall-trained shrub; good for mixed spring borders

**FLOWERS** February to March

**ASPECT** South, west or east facing, in a sheltered position; full sun to partial shade (flowering is reduced in shade)

**SOIL** Any fertile, well-drained soil

**HARDINESS** Fully hardy at temperatures down to -15°C/5°F; needs no winter protection (but late frost can damage young plants)

**DROUGHT TOLERANCE** Good, once established

**PROBLEMS** None

**CARE** Trim lightly after flowering; shorten the oldest branches by a third every five years to maintain size and shape

**PROPAGATION** Semi-ripe cuttings in summer; layering in summer

## Chimonanthus praecox
### Wintersweet

⬆ 4m/13ft ⬌ 3m/10ft                    EASY

This energetic, upright, deciduous shrub from China is famed for its delicate winter fragrance and it really brings a breath of cheer to the winter garden. It has lance-shaped mid-green leaves that open after the flowers. The slender, pale grey-green, bare stems are clustered with small, rounded, lemon-coloured flower buds, flushed pale pink at the base, opening to dangling, sweetly perfumed slightly cupped pale yellow flowers (2.5cm/1in across), stained plum in the interiors.

**BEST USES** Excellent in a mixed shrub border; ideal as a wall shrub for smaller gardens; makes a good specimen in a container; cut small flowering branches to scent rooms

**FLOWERS** December to February

**ASPECT** South, west or east facing, in a sheltered or exposed position; full sun

**SOIL** Any fertile, well-drained soil

**HARDINESS** Fully hardy at temperatures down to -15°C/5°F; needs no winter protection

**DROUGHT TOLERANCE** Excellent, once established

**PROBLEMS** None

**CARE** Remove any dead, diseased or damaged wood in late winter to early spring; if growing as a wall shrub, cut back to between 2–4 buds of the main branch framework after flowering

**PROPAGATION** Sow ripe seed immediately in pots in a cold frame; softwood cuttings in summer

## *Edgeworthia chrysantha*
### Paper bush

⬆ 1.5m/5ft ⬅➡ 1.5m/5ft            TRICKY

This rounded deciduous shrub is indigenous to the woodlands of China and the Himalayas and is related to the daphnes, so its fragrant qualities are cast iron. It has supple, cinnamon-coloured young stems and is clothed with dark green, lance-shaped leaves. The clusters of pale yellow flowers are heavily fragranced and open in late winter, before the foliage appears. Ensure you provide ideal conditions: this chap sulks if he isn't given what he wants (sounds like my other half!).

**BEST USES** Ideal for a shady border or woodland garden; good in containers against a warm wall in courtyard and patio gardens

**FLOWERS** February to March
**ASPECT** South, west or east facing, in a sheltered position; full sun to partial shade
**SOIL** Fertile, humus-rich, moist, well-drained loam
**HARDINESS** Frost hardy at temperatures down to -5°C/23°F; needs winter protection
**DROUGHT TOLERANCE** Good, once established
**PROBLEMS** None
**CARE** Cut out dead, diseased or damaged material as needed
**PROPAGATION** Semi-ripe cuttings in summer

........................................................

**GREENFINGER TIP** *This may struggle without the shelter of a south or west-facing wall*

## *Hamamelis mollis* 'Coombe Wood'
### Chinese witch hazel

⬆ 4m/13ft ⬅➡ 5m/16ft            EASY

Witch hazels are invaluable in winter and this open, multi-stemmed, spreading deciduous shrub is one of the most potently fragrant. It has smooth grey-brown bark and larger than average (over 15cm/6in long) spidery, saffron yellow, sweetly fragrant flowers, flushed red at the base, which explode open on the bare stems, like unexpected splashes of sunlight. Tiny, greenish capsules follow the flowers and the downy, mid-green leaves turn yellow in autumn.

**BEST USES** Great as a focal point in a lawn or mixed border; cut flowering twigs for indoor scent

**FLOWERS** January to February
**ASPECT** South or west facing, in a sheltered position with protection from cold winds; full sun to partial shade
**SOIL** Any fertile, well-drained soil; slight acidity is a bonus
**HARDINESS** Fully hardy at temperatures down to -15°C/5°F; needs no winter protection
**DROUGHT TOLERANCE** Excellent, once established
**PROBLEMS** Coral spot and honey fungus
**CARE** Minimal pruning; cut out dead, diseased or damaged wood as needed in winter
**PROPAGATION** Sow ripe seed immediately in pots in a cold frame

........................................................

**GREENFINGER TIP** *Don't be surprised if the flowers stay closed when the weather is overcast; they like a little sunny warmth to coax them out*

## *Lonicera fragrantissima*
### Shrubby honeysuckle

⬆ 2m/6ft ◀▶ 3m/10ft      EASY

Honeysuckles are commonly thought of as climbers, so this shrubby example may come as a surprise. However, this fast-growing, spreading, deciduous (semi-evergreen in mild areas) shrub from China is a gem. It has matt, rounded, pale green leaves, held in pairs on slender, arching stems that skirt the ground, and dainty, tubular, creamy white, lipped sweetly fragrant flowers from winter to spring. Rounded, small red berries follow the flowers. It can also be trained as a wall shrub or small climber, making it perfect for gardeners who are short of space.

**BEST USES** Excellent in a mixed shrub border; thrives in pots; grows well against a low wall or trellis; good for cottage and coastal gardens

**FLOWERS** November to March

**ASPECT** Any, in a sheltered or exposed position; full sun to partial shade

**SOIL** Any fertile, moist, well-drained soil

**HARDINESS** Fully hardy at temperatures down to -15°C/5°F; needs no winter protection

**DROUGHT TOLERANCE** Excellent, once established

**PROBLEMS** Aphids; powdery mildew

**CARE** Cut out dead, diseased or damaged wood after flowering

**PROPAGATION** Softwood cuttings in late spring to early summer; layering in spring

## *Lonicera* x *purpusii* 'Winter Beauty' 🎖
### Winter honeysuckle

⬆ 2m/6ft ◀▶ 2.5m/8ft      EASY

This rounded Chinese deciduous or semi-evergreen shrub has slender, red-brown stems that are studded with clusters of highly fragrant, lemon-scented creamy white flowers (2cm/¾in long) with distinctive, yellow anthers that hang upside down from the bare stems well in advance of the oval, dark green leaves. The foliage is pretty dull and it rarely produces berries like other honeysuckles, but we are talking heavenly fragrance in the depths of winter, and for that reason alone you should consider growing it.

**BEST USES** Ideal for clothing winter arbours; grow near the kitchen or living room window or by paths for the full effect of its delightful scent

**FLOWERS** December to March

**ASPECT** Any, in a sheltered or exposed position; full sun to partial shade

**SOIL** Any fertile, well-drained soil

**HARDINESS** Fully hardy at temperatures down to -15°C/5°F; needs no winter protection

**DROUGHT TOLERANCE** Good, once established

**PROBLEMS** None

**CARE** Prune in late spring, cutting out dead, damaged or diseased wood at the base of the plant to encourage new growth

**PROPAGATION** Semi-ripe cuttings in late summer

## *Sarcococca confusa* 🎖
### Sweet box

⬆ 2m/6ft ⬌ 90cm/3ft                    **EASY**

This is a neat, rounded, slow-growing evergreen shrub from China that is restrained in its growth habit and handsome too. It has dense foliage of elliptical, lustrous deep green leaves (some 6cm/2½in across). In winter, dainty, spidery, creamy white flowers are arranged along the length of the stems, perfuming the chill winter air with an intense vanilla fragrance. The flowers are followed by small, round, shiny black berries, which provide food for winter wildlife and encourage them into the garden. This is an ideal shrub for beginners, providing all-year interest with little maintenance.

**BEST USES** Excellent for shady city gardens; does well in containers; ideal for a gloomy border where little else will flourish; makes excellent low hedging; good for cutting and bringing indoors

**FLOWERS** December to March

**ASPECT** Any, in a sheltered position; partial to full shade

**SOIL** Any fertile, humus-rich, well-drained soil; tolerant of acid soil

**HARDINESS** Fully hardy at temperatures down to -15°C/5°F; needs no winter protection

**DROUGHT TOLERANCE** Excellent, once established

**PROBLEMS** None

**CARE** Cut out dead, diseased or damaged wood as needed, after flowering

**PROPAGATION** Semi-ripe cuttings in late summer

## *Viburnum* x *bodnantense* 'Dawn' 🎖

⬆ 3m/10ft ⬌ 2m/6ft                    **EASY**

This vigorous, rounded, deciduous shrub of garden origin is a fragrant winter delight. It has upright, pliable red stems with deep green, toothed leaves that arch outward with age, but it is the flowering on the bare stems that elevates this shrub above the norm. Pale pink buds open to very fragrant (almond and honey-scented) white-flushed pale pink tubular flowers and it blossoms madly: I have seen it flowering from October right through to Easter.

**BEST USES** Ideal for the mixed shrub and perennial border; useful as informal hedging

**FLOWERS** November to March

**ASPECT** Any, in a sheltered or exposed position; full sun to partial shade

**SOIL** Any fertile, moist, well-drained soil

**HARDINESS** Frost hardy at temperatures down to -5°C/23°F; needs winter protection

**DROUGHT TOLERANCE** Poor

**PROBLEMS** Viburnum beetle; honey fungus and leaf spot

**CARE** Deadhead to prolong flowering; lightly trim any flowering shoots to maintain size and shape in autumn, after final flowering

**PROPAGATION** Greenwood cuttings in early summer; hardwood cuttings in winter

**GREENFINGER TIP** *After a few years, cut back some of the older growth to ground level, to keep the shrub producing good flower displays*

## *Eriobotrya japonica* 🎖
### Loquat

⬆ 6m/20ft ↔ 4m/13ft　　　　　MEDIUM

Originally from China and Japan, this architectural plant is not widely grown and yet it is the most lovely large shrub or small tree and has much to commend it. The foliage is handsome: the large, glossy green, broadly oval leaves (30cm/12in long) are heavily veined on top, with white furry undersides. In winter, clusters of pale brown flower buds burst open to reveal small, white, exotically and extravagantly scented blossoms. And there's more: the seeds ripen to pendulous clusters of rounded, smooth egg-shaped, orange, aromatic fruits (4cm/1½in across) that have a sweet taste with a slight acidic edge (although the fruits rarely ripen in the UK, as they need long hot summers to mature).

> **BEST USES** Grow against a sunny, sheltered wall; happy in sheltered coastal gardens

**FLOWERS** November to March

**ASPECT** South or west facing, in a sheltered position with protection from cold winds; full sun

**SOIL** Any fertile, well-drained soil

**HARDINESS** Frost hardy at temperatures down to -5°C/23°F; needs winter protection

**DROUGHT TOLERANCE** Excellent, once established

**PROBLEMS** None

**CARE** Cut out dead, diseased or damaged wood in winter

**PROPAGATION** Semi-ripe cuttings in summer

## *Mahonia* x *media* 'Charity'
### Oregon grape

⬆ 5m/16ft ↔ 4m/13ft　　　　　EASY

This stiffly erect evergreen shrub of garden origin adds architectural shape to the fragrant winter garden. It has pale green stems with slightly spiny, serrated, paired, polished leaves (reminiscent of holly) and upright clustered spires of lightly lily of the valley-scented pale yellow flowers (up to 60cm/24in long). Black, acidic, rounded berries follow the flowers in spring. It is very low maintenance and ideal for the beginner. *M.* x *media* 'Winter Sun' 🎖 (4m/13ft height and spread) flowers from November to March.

> **BEST USES** Excellent as a focal point in a shady woodland border; good as informal hedging; useful ground cover on awkward slopes; pollution resistant, so does well in city roof gardens

**FLOWERS** November to January

**ASPECT** Any, in a sheltered or exposed position; partial shade

**SOIL** Any fertile, humus-rich, well-drained soil

**HARDINESS** Fully hardy at temperatures down to -15°C/5°F; needs no winter protection

**DROUGHT TOLERANCE** Excellent, once established

**PROBLEMS** Mildew and rust

**CARE** Cut out dead, diseased or damaged wood as needed, after flowering; cut back leggy stems to the base after flowering to encourage new, lower bushy growth

**PROPAGATION** Semi-ripe cuttings in late summer to early autumn

# Aromatic plants

There is a whole range of plants that do not have fragrant flowers but whose leaves are aromatic, releasing their scents when bruised or crushed. Most need little introduction: where would a cottage garden be without some lavender or a Mediterranean garden without rosemary? Many of these herbal plants have traditionally been used for culinary and medicinal purposes.

Aromatic plants are generally easier to grow than the fragrant plants that have spectacular flowers. Their foliage is unappealing to predators, so they tend to suffer less from pests, and they often have good resistance to disease. Many are Mediterranean in origin: these will thrive in fairly poor soils and have good drought tolerance.

## Agastache 'Black Adder' Hyssop

⬆ 90cm/3ft ⬌ 40cm/16in

A bushy, short-lived hardy perennial from arid terrains of Asia, Mexico and the USA with bristly, oval, pointed, mint-like liquorice-scented leaves and deep purple flower spikes with dense clusters of tiny, tubular, hazy violet flowers from July to October; grow in any well-drained soil, in full sun to partial shade, in a sheltered position; drought tolerant. A. 'Blue Fortune' is smaller, with mid-green nettle-like leaves and lilac-blue flower spires.

## Allium schoenoprasum Chives

⬆ 30–60cm/12–24in ⬌ 5cm/2in

A bulbous hardy perennial with edible, smooth, linear, dark green onion-scented leaves and tiny, star-shaped, pale purple flowers forming drumstick heads from July to August; grow in any well-drained soil, in full sun; drought tolerant.

## Allium tuberosum Garlic chives

⬆ 25–50cm/10–20in ⬌ 5cm/2in

A fast-growing frost-hardy bulbous perennial with edible, smooth, linear, dark green onion-flavoured leaves (about 35cm/14in long) and small clusters of star-shaped, fragrant white flowers from August to September; grow in any well-drained soil, in full sun; drought tolerant.

## Aloysia citrodora  Lemon verbena

⬆ 3m/10ft ⬌ 3m/10ft

A bushy, upright, frost-hardy shrub from South America with long, narrow, drooping, pointed mid-green leaves that smell of lemon sherbet when crushed; smooth, pinkish stems are topped with branching flower heads of tubular, star-shaped, pinky white flowers in August; grow in fertile to poor, well-drained soil, in full sun; drought tolerant.

## Angelica archangelica Angelica (below)

⬆ 2m/6ft ⬌ 1.2m/4ft

An architectural, fully hardy perennial (often grown as a biennial) from damp regions of Europe and Asia with tall, sturdy, ribbed green stems and deeply divided fresh green leaves, smelling of sweet dessert wine, and flattish domed flower heads of tiny, massed, zingy green-yellow flowers from June to July; grow in moist, fertile soil, in full sun to partial shade.

## Artemisia abrotanum  Lad's love

⬆ 90cm/3ft ⬌ 60cm/24in

A bushy, semi-evergreen shrub with deeply dissected, feathery, sage green musky-smelling leaves and small sprays of dirty yellow button flowers in August (it rarely flowers in the UK so is best grown as a foliage plant); grow in any well-drained soil, in full sun; drought tolerant.

## Artemisia absinthium 'Lambrook Mist'

⬆ 50cm/20in ⬌ 50cm/20in

A shrubby, evergreen, fully hardy perennial with feathery, sage grey aromatic foliage and insignificant grey-yellow flowers in August; grow in poor, well-drained soil, in full sun (withstands wet better than most); drought tolerant.

## Artemisia 'Powis Castle'
### Mugwort (below)

⬆ 90cm/3ft ⬌ 1.2m/4ft

A compact, woody-based, frost-hardy perennial with beautiful, finely filigreed, silver aromatic leaves with pale lemon flowers in August; grow in any well-drained soil, in full sun; drought tolerant.

## Borago officinalis Borage (right)

⬆ 60cm/24in ⬌ 45cm/18in

A bushy, strong-growing, fully hardy European annual with coarse, hairy, oval, matt green cucumber-scented leaves and branched stems with small bright blue flowers from June to October; grow in any well-drained soil, in full sun to partial shade; drought tolerant; invasive.

## Chaerophyllum hirsutum 'Roseum'
### Hairy chervil

⬆ 60cm/24in ⬌ 30cm/12in

An upright, clumping, deciduous, hardy perennial, found in meadows and hedgerows across Spain and France, that looks like a pink version of cow parsley, with ferny, bright green apple-scented leaves flushed plum, and slender, arching, reddish stems topped with massed umbels of tiny, soft pink flowers from April to June; unlike chervil (Myrrhis odorata), it has no culinary uses; grow in humus-rich soil, in full sun to partial shade. C. hirsutum has white flowers.

## Chamaemelum nobilis 'Flore Pleno'
### Chamomile

⬆ 15cm/6in ⬌ 45cm/18in

A carpeting hardy perennial from the Mediterranean, with small, ferny, mid-green fruit-scented leaves, studded with tiny, double, whitish green pompom-like flowers in July to August; grow in any well-drained soil, in full sun; very drought tolerant. C.n. 'Treneague' (10cm/4in x 45cm/18in) has tufted, fresh green aromatic foliage but is non-flowering and makes an excellent decorative lawn.

## Foeniculum vulgare Fennel

⬆ 2m/6ft ⬌ 45cm/18in

An architectural, fully hardy perennial that grows wild in meadows and roadsides all over southern Europe, with decorative, ferny, light green aniseed-scented foliage on smooth green stems and aromatic seed heads in autumn; its tiny yellow flowers are held on branching sprays from July to August; all parts of the plant have wide culinary use; grow in any fertile, well-drained soil, in full sun; drought tolerant. F.v. 'Purpureum' has bronze-burgundy foliage.

## Geranium macrorrhizum 'Bevan's Variety'

⬆ 50cm/20in ⬌ 60cm/24in

A spreading, rhizomatous, hardy perennial from temperate regions, with heavily lobed, evergreen, lemon-scented leaves and magenta pink-white flowers with pink stamens, in May to June; grow in any well-drained soil, in full sun to full shade; drought tolerant. *G.m.* 'Ingwersen's Variety' has pale pink flowers; *G.m.* 'Album' has white flowers, tinged pale pink.

## Helichrysum italicum  Curry plant

⬆ 60cm/24in ⬌ 90cm/3ft

A bushy, evergreen, frost-hardy shrub from Europe, with silver-grey stems and leaves that smell strongly of curry when bruised and sprays of small, brash, dark yellow flowers from July to September; grow in poor, well-drained soil, in full sun; drought tolerant.

## Laurus nobilis  Bay laurel/Sweet bay

⬆ 12m/40ft ⬌ 10m/32ft

An evergreen, frost-hardy conical tree or large shrub from the Mediterranean, with highly polished, oval, deep green leaves (up to 10cm/4in long) that are sweetly aromatic if rubbed or bruised, and clusters of small, pale yellow, shallow-cupped flowers in April to May, followed by small, rounded, black berries on female plants; grow in fertile, well-drained soil, in a sheltered position, in full sun to partial shade; drought tolerant. *L.n.* 'Aurea' has golden foliage.

## LAVANDULA Lavender

Lavenders are evergreen shrubs from the Mediterranean, famed for their silver-grey foliage and aromatic flower spikes, which are irresistible to bees. Most are fully hardy, and they usually flower from June to July. They come in different sizes and a large range of colours, including pink, white and yellow, as well as the more usual purples and blues. Lavenders thrive in dry, sunny climates: they enjoy poor, well-drained soil in full sun and are drought tolerant.

## Lavandula angustifolia 'Alba'

⬆ 30cm/12in ⬌ 30cm/12in

A compact, fully hardy variety with profuse white flowers.

## Lavandula angustifolia 'Hidcote'

⬆ 60cm/24in ⬌ 75cm/30in

A compact, bushy, strong-growing fully hardy variety, with silver-grey leaves and dark purple flowers; ideal for dwarf hedging.

## Lavandula stoechas  French lavender

⬆ 60cm/24in ⬌ 60cm/24in

A bushy, compact, fully hardy/borderline species with slightly unusual deep purple flowers topped with pale lilac winged flags.

## Lavandula stoechas subsp. stoechas f. rosea 'Kew Red' (below)

⬆ 45cm/18in ⬌ 60cm/24in

A half-hardy, compact plant with crimson flowers and creamy pink flags.

### *Leptospermum lanigerum* Woolly tea tree

⬆ 3–5m/10–16ft ⬌ 3m/10ft

An upright, loosely branching, frost-hardy evergreen shrub from Australia, with dense, oval, aromatic leaves with silky grey undersides and silvery grey young foliage, and a mass of shallow, bowl-shaped white flowers with interesting maroon-brown calyces from April to July, followed by woody fruits; grow in fertile, well-drained soil, in full sun to partial shade, with shelter from cold winds; drought tolerant; prune lightly after flowering.

### *Melissa officinalis* Lemon balm

⬆ 60cm–1.2m/2–4ft ⬌ 45cm/18in

A bushy, upright, fully hardy perennial from Europe, with oval, crinkled, serrated, light green lemon-scented leaves and flower spikes of small, pale yellow or whitish lipped flowers from June to October; grow in any well-drained soil, in full sun. *M.o.* 'Aurea' has gold-splashed leaves; *M.o.* 'All Gold' has vivid gold leaves.

### *Mentha* × *piperita* f. *citrata* Lemon mint

⬆ 50cm/20in ⬌ 90cm/3ft

A very vigorous, bushy, spreading, fully hardy perennial of garden origin with coarse, oval, dark green, lemon cologne-scented leaves, tinted burgundy-bronze when planted in shade, and spikes of whorled, tubular purple flowers in September; grow in any well-drained soil, from full sun to partial shade (grow in pots to prevent invasiveness). *M.* × *p.* f. *citrata* 'Chocolate' smells of chocolate mints, 'Grapefruit' is grapefruit scented and 'Orange' has orange scent.

### *Monarda* 'Cambridge Scarlet' 🏅
**Bee balm/Bergamot**

⬆ 90cm/3ft ⬌ 45cm/18in

A clump-forming, fully hardy herbaceous perennial from the North American prairies, with dark green pointed, oval, vein-etched, citrus-scented leaves and spidery, vivid red flowers, much-loved by bees and butterflies, from July to September; grow in any humus-rich, well-drained soil, in full sun to partial shade.

### *Myrrhis odorata* Sweet cicely/Chervil

⬆ 2m/6ft ⬌ 1.5m/5ft

A bushy, fully hardy herbaceous perennial from southern Europe, with decorative, edible, fresh green, ferny foliage that smells and tastes of aniseed, and branching clusters of tiny, starry, white flowers that are attractive to bees, from May to June, followed by edible, shiny dark brown seeds; grow in any moist, well-drained soil, in full sun to partial shade; self-seeds easily and can be invasive.

### *Nepeta* 'Six Hills Giant' Catmint

⬆ 90cm/3ft ⬌ 60cm/24in

A strong-growing, clump-forming, fully hardy perennial garden hybrid with narrow, pointed, lightly serrated, grey-green mint-scented leaves and upright green-grey stems with pastel lavender-coloured flower spikes from June to July; grows easily in any well-drained soil, in full sun to partial shade; drought tolerant.

### *Ocimum basilicum* Sweet basil

⬆ 60cm/24in ⬌ 30–60cm/12–24in

A bushy, short-lived perennial from across the Mediterranean, best grown as an annual, with elliptical, vivid green, slightly clove-scented leaves on vivid green upright stems and small flower spikes with clusters of white whorled flowers in August; grow in light, well-drained soil or in pots in a sheltered position, in full sun; pinch out the flower heads to keep the edible leaves productive.

### *Origanum vulgare* Oregano/Wild marjoram

⬆ 30–90cm/12–36in ⬌ 30–90cm/12–36in

A carpeting, fully hardy, woody-based perennial from the Mediterranean that spreads by rhizomes, with small, oval, stalkless, mid-green aromatic leaves and purple-tinted branching flower stems, with tiny, tubular purple flowers, loved by bees and butterflies, from June to September; grow in poor to fertile, well-drained soil, in full sun; drought tolerant. *O.v.* 'Aureum' 🏅 is less energetic (30cm/12in spread), with golden foliage and pink flowers in summer.

## Pelargonium 'Attar of Roses' ♙

⬆ 45cm/18in ⬌ 30cm/12in

A bushy, frost-tender evergreen perennial (often mistakenly called a geranium) of South African origin, with scallop-edged, light green rose-scented leaves on smooth, upright, apple-green stems, and small, simple, five-petalled pale pink flowers with fuchsia pink stamens, from June to August; grow in any well-drained soil, in full sun; drought tolerant. *P.* 'Chocolate Peppermint' has large, dark green, peppermint-scented leaves with chocolate-coloured markings and mauve flowers; *P.* (Fragrans Group) 'Fragrans Variegatum' (formerly 'Snowy Nutmeg') has variegated, grey-green nutmeg-scented leaves, with dainty white flowers.

## Prostanthera cuneata ♙  Mint bush

⬆ 30–90cm/12–36in ⬌ 30–90cm/12–36in

A bushy, spreading, woody-based, frost-hardy evergreen shrub from Tasmania, with loosely spreading upright green stems and small, shiny, rounded leaves that have a fresh minty smell when bruised, and long clusters of small, pretty, mint-scented, tubular white-lipped flowers, spotted with purple freckles inside, in July and August; grow in fertile, well-drained soil, in a sheltered position, in full sun.

## Rosa rubiginosa Sweet briar rose

⬆ 2.5m/8ft ⬌ 2.5m/8ft

A fast-growing, unruly, fully hardy deciduous shrub of native origin, with oval, crinkled, mid-green apple-scented leaves on prickly, arching stems, and pretty, lightly fragrant, shallow cupped pink blooms with golden stamens, from June to July, followed by vivid red hips in autumn; grow in fertile, humus-rich, well-drained soil, in full sun; drought tolerant.

## Rosmarinus officinalis Rosemary

⬆ 1.5m/5ft ⬌ 1.5m/5ft

A bushy, upright, fully hardy evergreen shrub from the Mediterranean, with blunt-needled, deep green aromatic foliage with whiter undersides, and tiny, tubular lavender flowers, from May to June; grow in any well-drained soil, in full sun; drought tolerant. *R.o.* 'Roseus' has unusual lilac-pink flowers; *R.o.* 'Tuscan Blue' (frost tender) has slightly broader, light green, nutmeg-scented leaves and dark blue flowers from May.

## Salvia elegans 'Scarlet Pineapple' (above)

⬆ 90cm/3ft ⬌ 50cm/20in

A branching, frost-tender herbaceous perennial with deeply vein-etched, heart-shaped, mid-green leaves, smelling of sage and pineapple, and tall, straight, slender, green stems bearing long, narrow, tubular vivid scarlet flowers, from August to September; grow in fertile, well-drained soil, in full sun to partial shade.

## Santolina pinnata subsp. neapolitana ♙

⬆ 75cm/30in ⬌ 90cm/3ft

A short-lived, dwarf, fully hardy evergreen shrub from the Mediterranean, with fine, ferny, grey-green aromatic foliage and button-like lemon flowers in June; grow in fertile to poor, well-drained soil, in full sun; drought tolerant.

## Thymus pulegioides 'Bertram Anderson' ♙
**Thyme**

⬆ 30cm/12in ⬌ 25cm/10in

A carpeting, fully hardy, woody-based evergreen shrublet from Europe with small, oval to elliptical, bright yellow-gold, lemon-scented leaves and masses of whorled lavender pink flowers, from June to July; grow in any well-drained soil, in full sun; drought tolerant.

## Thymus serpyllum 'Pink Chintz' ♙

⬆ 25cm/10in ⬌ 45cm/18in

A mat-forming, fully hardy evergreen shrub with small, bristly, grey-green leaves and tiny, whorled pastel pink flowers from June to July; grow in any well-drained soil, in full sun; drought tolerant.

# Planting with fragrant plants

Why are some plants scented and others not? Their means of pollination has much to do with it. Plants that are wind pollinated, such as ornamental grasses, don't need a scent to attract insect or animal pollinators: their pollen is carried on the breeze. Wind-pollinated plants are dowdy compared to the outrageously flirtatious flowering plants that rely on birds or insects for reproductive success.

Plants with boldly coloured flowers in bright reds and pinks can easily attract insects' attentions with their gaudy apparel. But pastel or white plants, which aren't giving off the 'sure thing' signals of the brightly coloured harlots, often have a secret weapon in their amorous armoury: sweet perfume. Many of the plants I've written about here have white or pale coloured flowers which often look fairly restrained – but they do smell wonderful.

There are plenty of unscented plants that offer extravagant blooms in bright colours, leaving the more modest fragrant plants to add their own special sensory dimension. Scented plants are as much about pleasurable memories and associations as they are about flowers or shapes. Bruised aromatic leaves or the whiff of pungent herbs tell us we've arrived in the kitchen garden; the waft of sweet peas heralds the arrival of summer and the heavenly perfumed roses summon romantic moments or pleasurable reminiscences of childhood. Flowers may be the glory of the garden but perfume remains their poetry.

An ideal plant will provide great foliage and attractive flowers as well as pleasant fragrance, but it is totally acceptable to choose a scented plant just because it has a lovely smell, even if its other features are a little dull. This is particularly true in winter, which offers a secret cache of scented shrubs. These may not be flamboyant in flower, but their perfume packs a punch on a cold winter's day, unchallenged by the myriad perfumes that dizzily intoxicate in the summer months. And sometimes an evocative smell is an unintended surprise from a plant that is serving another function altogether, such as making an evergreen hedge or screen.

Plants that have sweet, spicy or exotic fragrance are doing their best to attract bees, butterflies, beetles or night-flying moths – and their attractiveness to these insects is yet one more reason for choosing to grow fragrant plants. Some plants have fouler scents; these are relying on low-life lotharios such as flies and bluebottles for their breeding success. They have not been included in this book, as the smell of rotting carrion (which is common among such plants) is not bewitching to the twitching nostril.

## The shopping list

Using scented plants in the garden needs careful thought. A few fragrant plants can go a long way, but they will be taking their place in the garden among a host of glorious plants with strong visual appeal.

First, consider the atmosphere you are trying to create. You may love the rough and tumble cottage-garden style with billowing roses and honeysuckle. Or perhaps you have a very austere modern garden with clean, crisp lines but want to introduce fragrance in keeping with a contemporary style of planting. Keep this vision in mind while making more detailed plans.

Next, assess the garden space and planting areas. Look at the aspect (see page 96) and the soil (see page 97) and then spend a few evenings leafing through gardening books and magazines, making a list of the plants (scented and unscented) that catch your eye. Note how big each plant will grow and whether you have the right soil and location for it: if not, be ruthless and cross it off the list.

Now consider the colour choices, imagining which ones are going to complement the flowers in your garden. Whites, blues, pale yellows and pinks all work well together. Or maybe the bold oranges of hemerocallis or the deep purple and vibrant reds of rhododendrons have more appeal for you.

Pay close attention to the flowering periods. If you choose three scented plants that flower at the same time and plant them close together, the olfactory experience will be overwhelming. By choosing plants that flower in succession, you are more likely to end up with a steady release of fragrance – as one scent fades, another takes over. And spacing scented plants a reasonable distance apart (at least 2m/6ft) will allow the nose some respite.

Think also of plant shapes and leaf colour. Ensure you have spreading, mound-forming plants as well as vertical ones to create interest in the border. Choose a few plants that are architectural or structural in appearance, to create focal points in the border. It is a real bonus to find a fragrant plant that has great foliage. Try to mix large-leaved plants with others that have smaller foliage. And how about those that offer interesting flower shapes, and seed heads or berries after flower? A plant that offers fragrance, foliage and seed heads, such as some of the few fragrant clematis, is going to provide a long season of interest.

If you are just beginning to plant a new garden, pop down to the local nursery or garden centre and pick out all the plants on your list (assuming there are not too many). Arrange them on one of the pathways and stand back. How do they look together? Are the heights, shapes, leaves and colours complementary? This is incredibly useful in helping you visualise the likely end result once everything is planted. And if the plants are in flower, it is also a good opportunity to

A blue haze of scented lavender in summer: fragrant plants encourage beneficial insects into your garden

The scent of jasmine intensifies in the cool of evening

three of each perennial will have more impact. Plant in groups of odd numbers for an informal effect, and in even numbers for a more formal appearance.

## Planning a scented garden

How do you decide where to put your scented plants? Position them for your own private pleasure, in places where you can best appreciate their fragrance. Plant a scented shrub or climber under a window so you can enjoy a draught of its sweet perfume as you go about the day's chores. A floral scent on a grey winter's day will lift your mood: one (or more) of the many scented viburnums by the front path will provide that seasonal boost.

Some shrubs, such as honeysuckles and jasmines, become more fragrant in the evening, as the light fades and the temperature cools. Sheltered areas that are seldom stirred by a breath of air will contain a powerful scent very effectively, so a courtyard or seating space where you like to unwind on a balmy evening is the perfect spot to plant one or more of the night-scented plants. This is when the pale colours of the many desirable evening wafters come into their own, taking on a shining luminosity in the twilight.

Common sense suggests that herbs grown in pots are best sited somewhere near the kitchen door, and you may also have the space to grow herbs in their own raised beds or in a herb garden or parterre, creating an aromatic haven. Be warned that some herbs, such as mints, comfrey and lemon balm, just don't know their place and can become very invasive. These are best grown in pots unless you can give them a space to themselves.

A hot sunny border is an excellent place to grow the lovely aromatic shrubs, such as cistus, rosemary and lavender. Some scented shrubs will really benefit from being planted in shady beds, and they can be underplanted

check that you like their smell. Visiting the many private houses that open their gardens is another good way of gathering ideas for new planting schemes and seeing desirable plants in situ.

Now, exercising a fair amount of restraint (which is always hard, but necessary), edit the list again. Pare down your choices so that you end up with a smaller number of plants that flower in succession. Look at the list again. Presumably there are fewer colour and scent clashes. Go with those.

How many plants do you need? It rather depends on whether you are adding scent to an existing scheme, or starting from scratch. A couple of plants will be enough to fill any gaps but if the space is woefully bereft of planting you will need many more. Single plants of many different varieties are not very effective: planting a group of at least with scented flowering bulbs such as snowdrops, daffodils, hyacinths and iris for a fragrant spring.

Vertical spaces such as house walls and outbuildings provide the ideal habitat for many a scented climber and are space-saving in smaller gardens. Unsightly fencing is perfect for a sprawling honeysuckle – and why not throw in a scented rose for good measure? A late spring-flowering honeysuckle and a summer-flowering fragrant rose will combine beautifully, providing a continuous stream of scent for two months or more. An arch, pergola or trellis cries out for a fragrant partner. These are perfect spots for a fragrant clematis, smaller climbing roses, honeysuckle, jasmine or wisteria.

Don't overlook the obvious natural supports in your garden. There may be a tree that looks dull once its main flowering period is over. If it could take the weight of one of the more vigorous climbers such as a rambling rose or wisteria, this would lengthen its season of interest. Avoid putting a timorous grower against a rampant tree or shrub (or vice versa) as one will undoubtedly outgrow or swamp the other. Pair moderate growers with other scented climbing plants of the same growth rate.

Check that the climber won't outgrow the space you have to offer it. So, if you are looking for a climbing rose to grow in a container in a small town garden, don't pick a rambler: it may be small when you buy it, but could easily end up topping 6m/20ft. On the other hand, climbers or shrubs that are a bit sensitive will never attain their expected height if they are planted in an exposed spot, so find them somewhere sheltered from cold winds.

Trees and shrubs need to be sited with care from the outset. They will become permanent features in the garden and, unlike perennials, they cannot be easily moved. Don't be afraid to ask a nursery for advice about rates of growth and expected heights and spreads. A tree, shrub or hedge does not stop growing once it has reached the height you want: it will keep growing at the same rate unless you put in the effort to keep it at a manageable height. Think twice, plant once.

It would be folly to pick a tree or large shrub for its scented properties alone, so think about other features, such as shape: mounding, rounded, conical, spreading, ground hugging or weeping. Shrubs can be used creatively as hedging or for purely ornamental purposes, planted in a boundary, border or shrubbery. A slow-growing shrub may be just right for making a division in a garden – if it's fragrant, too, why waste a heaven-sent opportunity to provide both amenity and pleasure? An evergreen hedge can be used to create privacy or hide an unsightly landmark – and if you choose osmanthus or one of the evergreen viburnums you have fragrance and practicality in complete harmony.

Roses grown up walls can bring wafts of perfume through open doors and windows

# Aspect

## Sun and shade

Some plants need full sun to thrive, while others may be far happier in partial or full shade, so it is important to know how much sun and shade your garden enjoys when choosing which plants to buy and deciding where to plant them.

The direction your garden faces (north, south, east or west) is referred to as its aspect. In the northern hemisphere, a garden that faces south will be in full sun all day (at least when the sun is shining), while a garden with a north-facing aspect will receive only indirect sunlight, or be in shade for much of the day. East-facing beds catch the morning sun, and those facing west are likely to be sunny in the afternoon and evening.

For most of us, the position of our garden borders comes with the house, but if you have a choice, site your borders against a west or south-facing wall or fence. The old saying 'west is best' has some foundation in truth, as this is probably the best of all options for growing a wide range of plants. North-facing spaces are notorious trouble spots, receiving precious little sunlight, but there are a great many plants that can cope admirably with partial or full shade. As a general rule, large-leaved and woodland plants will thrive in gloomier conditions. Planting in raised beds, or even placing planted pots on a table or on a plant stand in the garden will help them get their heads nearer the light in shady gardens.

Nearby buildings and trees cast shade, especially in built-up areas and cities, where surrounding buildings often block the sunlight. This can change the local conditions, so don't take it for granted that a south-facing town garden will be drenched in sunshine. Garden sheds, outbuildings and garages may also create shady areas. Take some time to become familiar with the pattern of sunshine and shade in your own garden at different times of day and over the different seasons. Choose a plant that likes your particular conditions and you stand the best chance of growing success.

## Shelter

Brick walls, fencing and hedges or mature trees and shrubs all provide shelter in a garden. These boundaries will protect your garden plants against strong, cold or drying winds. Gardens without shelter take the full brunt of winds, hard rain, frosts, and snow in winter and drying winds and glaring, direct overhead sunlight in the summer months.

Every garden has its own microclimates. A sunny wall that enjoys long sunshine hours will have warmer soil at its footings and rarely be exposed to any winds at all, providing a sheltered environment for a less hardy plant. Greenhouses, cold frames, polytunnels and conservatories are controlled, sheltered environments, where plants are protected from the harsher elements of our climate. In mild areas and city centres, frosts are not going to be a major problem, whereas gardeners who live in colder regions where hard winter frosts are par for the course will struggle to grow some of the more tender plants.

Exposed gardens, including coastal gardens whose main adversary is salt and wind, have to deal with the extremes of winter weather and summer heat. It is essential to provide some sort of windbreak to protect your plants, otherwise you are going to struggle to grow anything meaningful. Walls and fences or hedging will filter out the worst of the weather so your plants can establish happily.

# Soil

Plants need soil to grow: it anchors them in the ground and provides them with the essential nutrients, air and water they need. Different plants grow better in different soils, so matching the soil to the plant is a major factor in growing any plant successfully.

## Types of soil

There are four common types of garden soil – sandy, clay, loam and chalk – and they differ in their ability to retain water, their nutrient values and in their acidity or alkalinity.

**Sandy** soil is light, dry, well-aerated soil that is free draining and easy to dig. Because water drains through it so quickly and nutrients are easily washed away, sandy soil improves when enriched with organic matter, which helps it retain moisture and improves fertility. However, plants that struggle in heavy, waterlogged soils, such as lavender and rosemary, will thrive in unimproved sandy soil.

**Clay** soils are wet and heavy to dig in winter but rock hard in times of drought. The soil texture is heavy and condensed, and aeration is poor, so many plants struggle to get their roots down into clay. It is slow to warm up in spring, but retains warmth well once the growing season is underway. On the plus side, clay soil is high in nutrients and supports a wider selection of plants, trees and shrubs than almost any other soil. These include echinacea, hemerocallis, lilacs, mock orange, roses and wild primroses.

**Loam** is rich, dark brown in colour, allowing it to absorb the heat of the sun easily, and has a crumbly texture. It has all the good points of clay and sandy soils, without any of their disadvantages. It is easy to dig, has high nutrient levels, good water retention and plant roots become easily established. Almost all trees, shrubs and perennials, except acid-lovers, will appreciate loam.

**Chalk** (or limestone) soils are very free draining and lack fertility, as nutrients simply get washed away. They can be dry in summer and sticky and difficult to work on in winter. Adding organic matter annually is the only reliable method of improving chalky soils. There are many lime-hating plants, so planting choices can be limited, but aquilegias, peonies, rosemary, santolina and viburnums will succeed in chalky soils.

The soil's **acidity** or **alkalinity** can affect your choice of plants. It is measured as pH, on a scale of 1–14; soil with a pH of 7 is said to be neutral, below 7 is acid and above 7 is alkaline (buy a simple kit to test your soil's pH value). Most plants will grow on a pH between 6 and 7, so you don't need to worry about it too much, but some plants are acid-lovers and can't thrive in neutral soils; these are known as ericaceous plants. Avoid them if you have neutral or alkaline soil.

## Improving the soil

The soil that comes with your garden is unlikely to be an ideal crumbly loam, but with a little effort it is easy enough to transform unpromising soil into something in which a wide range of plants, shrubs and trees can thrive. Regular application of organic matter such as well-rotted farmyard manure, mushroom compost, leafmould or garden compost will improve the structure

Bergamot thrives in humus-rich, well-drained soil

- **sandy soil** – dig in organic matter
- **clay soil** – dig in grit; dig in organic matter or spread on the surface
- **compacted soil** – dig in grit, and organic matter if needed; rotovate to break up the compacted surface layer
- **wet soil** – dig in grit or gravel; if the soil is very wet, consider digging soakaways, ditches or drains, or plant in raised beds

Do this every year for three or four years and the condition of your soil – and thus the quality of the plants you grow in it – will improve 100 per cent. Once the soil is in a workable condition, you can drop back to a more leisurely regime, treating the soil once every two to three years.

## Organic soil improvers

As plants grow, they draw on nitrogen in the soil and this needs to be replenished. Nature normally does this for us, but as gardeners we interrupt the process by removing dead leaves, debris and lawn trimmings, which would normally break down to replenish nitrogen supplies. Organic soil improvers replace this lost material.

**Farmyard manure** is available by the bag in garden centres. In rural areas, animal owners sell it at low cost, but it must be well rotted before it is used in the garden (black, and with little or no smell). If it is still light-coloured and reeking of ammonia, wait for it to rot down: it can scorch or kill your plants if added in this state.

Apply in spring to sandy soils and in autumn on clay soil. If the soil is really waterlogged or compacted, dig it in to the top 30cm/12in, to help speed up the process in the first year. Otherwise spread a thick blanket (5–8cm/2–3in) right across the beds or put individual spadefuls around trees, shrubs and perennials, and leave nature to do the work.

of the soil and is particularly beneficial to light sandy soils, chalky and clay soils. Chemical fertilisers give plants a short-term boost, but they do not improve the structure or fertility of the soil and are not a substitute for organic matter.

Adding organic matter improves drainage and aeration, making the soil easier to manage; it increases the fertility of the soil, providing nutrients for the plants and encouraging good root establishment; and it helps hold moisture in the soil, which is invaluable during periods of dry weather, making plants less vulnerable to the effects of drought.

Digging grit or pea shingle into heavy clay soil will open it up, allowing plants to get their roots down without difficulty and water and air to penetrate more freely.

Soil improvement is best done in late winter or early spring, when the cold weather and frosts will help break down the organic material into the soil. But doing it at any time of year is better than not doing it at all.

**Mushroom compost** will improve the structure of heavy clay soils and add humus to thin sandy or chalky soils. It is very light in weight, making it easy to handle. Normally mushroom compost is pH neutral, but it should not be used for ericaceous (lime-hating) plants.

Apply to the surface of the soil as a mulch, layering it about 5–8cm/2–3in thick, in late winter or early spring on sandy soils or in autumn or winter on heavy clay soils.

**Leafmould** is decayed leaf matter and is rich in humus, beneficial bacteria and micro-organisms. It adds bulk to the soil and improves its texture. To make leafmould, collect fallen leaves into a bin liner or wire mesh bin, water them when they are dry, and leave for a year or two.

Dig in leafmould to bulk up sandy soil and open up clay soil, or spread over the soil as a conditioner. Use leafmould that is extremely well-rotted for potting plants and seed sowing by mixing it with equal parts of sharp sand, loam and garden compost.

**Garden compost** is decaying plant matter, collected together and left to rot down. It is an efficient way to recycle plant waste, and adds bulk and nutrients to the soil.

A compost heap (or two) is an ideal way to make garden compost. Compost bins, made in tough plastic or slatted wood, are an alternative. They vary in capacity, but 300 litres (66 gallons) is probably the minimum size to meet the needs of an average garden. For a tiny city garden, a small wooden or plastic composter that slots neatly into a corner will make enough compost for potting up plants or mulching new plants.

Site your heap or bin in sun or partial shade and somewhere that is easy to access with a wheelbarrow, with heaps placed directly on the soil or grass. You will need a lid or cover for the top: an old carpet will do, or you can buy tough, stretchy covers.

Any plant matter will compost eventually, but brown, woody material takes longer to rot down than green, leafy material. When making compost, use roughly equal amounts of green and brown material, but don't include infected plants or perennial weeds such as bindweed, buttercups and dandelions; nettles are an exception, as they help the heap rot down more quickly. Avoid substances that attract vermin (food) or don't rot down (ashes, tins).

Green material includes grass clippings, soft green plant stems and leaves, spent bedding plants, vegetable peelings and any non-woody prunings, as well as teabags and coffee grounds. Brown material includes cardboard, crushed eggshells, shredded paper, straw, wood shavings and tough hedge clippings (chop up woody material).

## MAKING COMPOST

There are two compost-making methods: compost made in 'hot' heaps is ready to use within a few months, but needs a large amount of material at the start; 'cool' heaps take longer to rot down, but can be built up gradually.

*Hot heaps* Make a thick base layer of woody plants or twigs and then fill the bin or build the heap with equal amounts of well-mixed brown and green material, watering as you go. Cover and leave to heat up. After two or three weeks, turn the heap with a fork, mixing everything thoroughly, and add water if it has dried out. Leave for several months. The compost is ready for use when it is dark brown and crumbly, and smells earthy (don't worry about the odd lump or twig).

*Cool heaps* Make a twiggy base, as above, and add a layer of mixed green and brown material. Add further layers as material becomes available. Over time the top layer will sink as the material below begins to rot. If you have the time, turning the contents of the heap with a fork will speed the process up enormously. It will be at least a year before the compost is ready to use.

# Growing

There are a wide range of plants in this book, from herbaceous perennials and bulbs to shrubs and small trees. They have different growing needs, but almost all are easy-going plants that need little maintenance. However, without exception, they need light, water and certain minimum temperatures to thrive happily.

**Herbaceous perennials** are soft-stemmed plants with ornamental flowers that live for more than a year, producing new growth and flowers each successive year. Perennials grown in this country are usually hardy or half hardy and most are easy to care for. They need little maintenance other than cutting back to ground level in autumn or early spring.

**Bulbous plants** (bulbs, corms and rhizomes) are perennials that have developed their own storage chambers containing all the nutrients each potential plant needs to complete its life cycle. They are usually bought and planted when dormant, and they disappear underground once they have flowered.

**Trees and shrubs** are a more permanent part of the garden than perennials. In the wild, mature shrubs and trees are able to cope without help, and the same applies in the garden if they are well cared for when young. Shrubs may need some pruning, to keep them flowering at their best and to prevent them growing too large, but otherwise they can look after themselves.

**Climbers** are simply plants that climb, and include perennials and wall shrubs. Most of them need some form of support to help them climb, and some also need annual pruning.

## Buying

Try to avoid the temptation to buy on impulse. If you plan ahead and make a list, you are more likely to buy a plant that earns its keep and suits your soil or garden aspect.

**Container-grown plants** Many plants (particularly herbaceous perennials and climbers, but also shrubs and trees) are sold in pots. They can be kept in their pots for as long as necessary (which could be a year or more). Just keep them well watered.

Pots vary in size. Larger plants have more immediate impact but smaller plants are much cheaper and can also be easier to establish: it is surprising how quickly a plant grows once it is planted in the ground.

Day lilies (*Hemerocallis dumortieri*) are easy to grow and have great flower shape and foliage

## GROWING BULBS

Bulbs are rather miraculous. They may look unpromising, but each one is a food and water storage chamber for a dormant plant. Contained in its fleshy root are all the ingredients it needs to transform into a thing of beauty.

**Buying** Ensure bulbs are plump and firm to the touch and not squashy, dried out or soft with mildew. Many bulbs deteriorate when left out of the ground, so try to plant them soon after buying.

**Planting** Bulbs need good drainage; they will rot in waterlogged conditions. Plant spring-flowering bulbs in September, summer-flowering bulbs in spring and autumn-flowering bulbs in summer (with the exception of snowdrops, which are usually dug up in early spring as they are beginning to die back and replanted straight away).

If you are planting into a flowerbed, dig in some fertiliser or bonemeal. Make a series of holes, planting bulbs as you go. Obvious as it may seem, plant bulbs the right way up. The pointed tip should face skywards, with the flattened basal plate pushed firmly into the soil.

As a general rule of thumb, plant bulbs to a depth of at least two to three times their size. Some bulbs, such as crinums, are planted with the 'nose' or tip of the bulb breaking the soil: these bulbs flower better when they are baked in summer, rather than kept cool and moist underground.

Once flowering is over, let bulb leaves die back naturally. Never cut them back or tie them in knots: this prevents them building up food stores for the following year. All fully hardy bulbs can be left in the ground, provided the soil is well drained. You may lose a few bulbs each year to squirrels and mice, but most bulbs left underground will survive and gradually increase in number.

**Storing** Less hardy species (including most summer-flowering bulbs) need to be lifted and stored through the winter. Dig them up once the foliage has yellowed, and discard damaged bulbs. Clean off loose soil, remove decaying foliage and leave them to dry for a week in a shed or airing cupboard, before storing and labelling them in shallow trays or brown paper bags in a cool, dry, frost-free spot. Dusting them lightly with fungicide will help prevent disease. Replant the following year. Alternatively, buy fresh bulbs each year.

**Forcing** Scented bulbs are ideal for 'forcing' (bringing into flower early indoors), giving a delightful reminder of spring while it is still winter outside. Hyacinths and small narcissi are commonly forced for their scent.

In early autumn, place a layer of hyacinth bulbs on potting compost or bulb fibre in pots or containers, ensuring the sides don't touch. Fill the pots with more compost, leaving the tips of the bulbs peeping through, and move to a cool, dark place. Keep the compost just moist and leave for 8–10 weeks, until the shoots begin to emerge, then bring into a warm, light room. Expect flowers about a month later.

Pot up daffodils as for hyacinths, but leave their tips just below the compost surface. They need more light than hyacinths so, when the shoots appear, place them on a warm windowsill until they flower. After flowering they can be replanted outside in a sunny sheltered spot.

It is important to buy disease-free plants. Look for fresh green leaves that aren't blotched or discoloured and make sure stems are undamaged. Check that the roots aren't escaping through the bottom of the pot. If the plant is not too big, up-end it into your hand: the roots should be white and healthy and not wrapping themselves round in circles. Press your thumb into the surface of the compost to see if it is moist and spongy. Weeds in the compost are a sign of neglect, so pass those by.

A small, bushy, balanced plant will grow into a more attractive shape than one that is tall and lopsided. Choose a plant with plenty of flower buds, rather than an appealing mass of open blooms that will soon fade.

**Bare-root plants** Deciduous trees, shrubs and roses are often bought 'bare root'. Grown in a field and dug up with only a small amount of soil clinging to their roots, they are sold in the dormant season, from autumn to early spring, when they have no leaves and are not in active growth. They are vulnerable to drying out and need to be replanted promptly. Bare-root plants establish quicker than more mature potted trees and shrubs, and they are very much cheaper than plants grown in containers.

When buying, look for healthy, balanced plants with well-developed roots; if the roots are dry and wizened, choose another one. If you are planning to buy a particular species or cultivar for planting in pairs, or as an avenue or hedge, check that the nursery has enough in stock. The plants need to be more or less identical in height and girth.

**Where to buy?** Garden centres are the obvious place to find plants locally, but bare-root plants are more widely available from specialist nurseries (look in the *RHS Plant Finder* for relevant nurseries). Nurserymen and women have a wealth of knowledge that they are happy to share, so don't be shy of asking for guidance. A nursery can often suggest a new cultivar that may out-perform your chosen tree or shrub in terms of bark, colour, habit or flowering.

Most specialist nurseries have mail order or online facilities, but some of my best plants have been bagged at markets and garden open days, with the odd cutting from friends.

## Planting

**Container-grown plants** can be planted at almost any time of year, though autumn to spring is ideal. Avoid planting when the ground is frozen or waterlogged. If you are planting through the summer, keep plants well watered.

Choose a suitable place for your plant, bearing in mind its future size, and check that this has the right aspect and soil. Certain plants dislike cold or drying winds,

### CONTAINER PLANTING

Gardening in containers is ideal if you have very little outdoor space, but pots and containers also have a place in larger gardens, where they can make effective focal points or highlight a particular plant. Almost anything can be grown in a container, as long as it does not grow too large.

Lay crocks (pieces of broken terracotta pot) at the bottom of the container, over the drainage holes, to prevent soil becoming waterlogged. Lifting pots off the ground with pot feet also helps with drainage. Where weight might be an issue, for large pots on balconies and roof terraces, fill a third of the pot with pieces of polystyrene before filling the container with compost.

Fill the pot with compost, leaving a gap of about 2.5cm/1in at the top of the pot to allow space for watering. Most perennials are happy with multi-purpose compost, but avoid using old compost as its nutrients will be exhausted and it may contain weed seed. Mixing water-swelling granules with the compost will reduce the watering regime from every day (without the granules) to once or twice a week. Plant as you would when planting into the ground, ensuring the plant is firmed in well, and keep well watered. The compost should feel damp to the touch.

Plants in containers use all the nutrients in the soil each year, so top up the soil annually with organic matter. Alternatively, thumb in small cones of slow-release fertiliser. A handful of pelleted chicken manure, scattered on the soil surface and watered in, is perfect for keeping potted plants well fed.

so provide them with a sheltered spot, but remember that the earth at the bottom of walls is notoriously dry, and may have concrete footings; plant climbers 30–90cm/12–36in away from the wall and angle the plant towards it.

Plants appreciate a good drink before planting. Dunk the plant, pot and all, in a bucket of water for half an hour, so the water really saturates the roots. Dig a hole about the same size as the pot and large enough to accommodate the rootball easily. Break up the soil in the bottom of the planting hole as this helps the roots to establish, and throw a generous handful of compost or other organic matter into the planting hole.

Turn the plant upside down, cupping the foliage with your hand for support, and gently ease the plant from the pot. Pot-grown plants often have roots that are tightly bound and wrapped in circles: gently tease them apart before putting them into the planting hole.

Position the plant so that the compost is level with the surrounding soil (clematis and roses are exceptions to this general rule: see pages 114 and 35). Backfill with soil, firm around the plant and water again. Dress the base of the plant with a thick ring of organic matter about 5cm/2in deep after planting.

**Bare-root plants** are planted in the dormant season, before they start growing. If it is not convenient to plant them immediately, bury the roots in a temporary trench. Plants will keep for some weeks like this so long as the roots are not allowed to dry out.

Plant individual plants in the same way as plants grown in pots (see above). Dig a hole deep enough to spread the roots out, water the roots well, backfill and stake as necessary (see below). An annual mulch of well-rotted manure, about 5cm/2in thick, at the base of new shrubs and trees will make sure the plants establish well.

Reduce the height of bare-root shrubs by half immediately after planting. This may seem drastic, but I have found that they grow stronger and bushier when they are cut back.

## Supporting plants

Many plants need additional support as they grow. Always use soft string, raffia or garden twine when tying young plants to supports, to prevent damage to the plant stem.

**Herbaceous perennials** Staking stops tall, floppy plants falling sideways and crushing their neighbours. Some plants never reach any great height, or are reasonably self-supporting, so staking isn't necessary, but many herbaceous perennials need support.

All sorts of plant supports are available, from bamboo canes and twiggy pea-sticks to

Spring bulbs being planted in the autumn

---

**PLANTING A HEDGE**

Trees, conifers or shrubs planted close together in a line form a hedge. They will establish best if planted in autumn or spring when the soil is warm, encouraging healthy root development.

Weed the planting area thoroughly and peg a string along the planting line. Dig a series of holes, about 30–60cm/12–24in apart, or dig a continuous trench for bare-root plants. Line the holes or trench with some well-rotted manure and fork in lightly. Plant as above, keeping the plants straight and upright, and ensuring the bases of the stems are not buried.

After planting, cut back the lead shoots and lateral stems by a third in May to encourage bushy growth. Clip hedges regularly to restrict their size and height. Keep the base of the hedge weed free and water regularly in the first year or two, particularly in dry periods. Mulch with organic matter annually in spring.

## SUPPORTS FOR CLIMBERS AND WALL SHRUBS

A few climbers are fully self-supporting but many are not. Climbers can be grown on trellis or wires, attached to walls and fences, or up sturdy free-standing structures such as pillars and pergolas, arbours and archways. Wall shrubs will happily grow upwards with support from trellis or wires, and climbing and rambling roses are often trained along wires, to improve their flowering (see page 36). Tie stems in as they grow, using garden twine, raffia or rose ties.

Install plastic-coated or galvanised wires on a wall or fence before planting, using vine eyes or tension bolts placed no more than 2m/6ft apart, with the first horizontal wire about 45cm/18in above ground level and further wires 30–45cm/12–18in apart. Ensure the wires are tensioned and pulled as tightly as possible.

When fixing trellis, mount it on wooden battens to create a gap between trellis and wall. This will ensure good air circulation and help to reduce diseases.

decorative wrought-iron or plastic-coated metal obelisks and wigwams. Stake plants when planting: it is easy to forget later, and plants look cramped and choked if they are staked when fully grown. Push canes deep into the ground near the plant or position support structures over the plants so they can grow through them. Most perennials do not need tying in.

**Trees and shrubs** Most shrubs can support themselves, but wall shrubs need tying in to a framework of trellis or wires (see box). Young trees need staking for the first few years after planting. Staking prevents winds rocking their roots, helping them to establish strongly.

Keep tree stakes as low as possible, and certainly no higher than two-thirds the height of the tree. Drive the stake into the open planting hole at an angle in the direction of the prevailing wind. The stake must be driven in firmly or it will not support the tree, but never hammer it through the rootball, as this will damage the roots. Leave about 2.5cm/1in between the tree trunk and the stake to allow the tree some movement while it establishes. Tie the tree to the stake with a rubber or plastic tree tie, to avoid damaging the bark. Large trees may need more than one stake.

Ornamental structures add instant vertical interest to borders, providing climbing apparatus for fragrant climbers

# Mulching

Annual mulching with organic matter is probably the single most important task in the garden. It improves the structure of the soil, which in turn improves its drainage, fertility and water retention, allowing plants to grow stronger and healthier and flower more exuberantly. Feed your soil, and you will rarely, if ever, have to feed your plants.

Spread a 5cm/2in layer of organic matter over the whole flowerbed or make a collar of mulch around individual plants, avoiding the stems. Apply in late autumn or early spring (or indeed whenever you remember), ensuring the ground is not bone dry or frozen. This will keep the nutrition levels in the soil high, so that they are available to your plants throughout the year.

Sandy and chalk soils need annual mulching unless you want to grow plants in them that prefer poor soil. Clay soil will also benefit. After four years of annual mulching, my heavy sticky clay became pretty

manageable; I then mulched it only every two or three years. Give it a go: it seems like hard work at the time, but it will pay dividends.

Mulching with either organic or inorganic materials has other advantages. Applied to moist soil, a mulch traps moisture at the roots where it can be taken up by the plant more effectively and prevents water evaporating from the soil surface. It also prevents weed emergence, by blocking out light to weed seed waiting to germinate. A dark mulch absorbs the warmth of the sun, which will result in better root establishment. Last but not least, some mulches look good.

# Watering

Mulching is top of the list for water conservation (see above), but it is also important to preserve water where we can. Place water butts around the garden or near guttering and downpipes from the house or greenhouse to catch rainwater. In addition, water in the early morning or late evening, when there is less risk of wastage from evaporation.

The amount of time you spend watering depends entirely on the size of your garden and what you are growing. Pots and containers dry out quickly and need almost daily watering unless you are using water-swelling granules (which can reduce watering to once or twice weekly).

Flowerbeds that are full of herbaceous perennials may need watering two or three times a week, and more often in dry weather – sometimes every day. However, if you have a good many drought-tolerant plants, you can probably go for two weeks or more before having to worry.

A thorough drenching lasting minutes is preferable to one that lasts only a few seconds. If you aren't sure whether you've watered enough, press your finger into the

---

## MULCHING

*Organic mulches* include well-rotted farmyard manure, mushroom and garden compost, leafmould and grass clippings (see page 99). Bark chippings can have the counter-effect of robbing nitrogen from the soil while they are rotting down, so they are not useful as a nutritious mulch.

*Inorganic mulches*, such as pebbles, shingle, slate, river stones or marble and glass chippings, are long lasting and ornamental, but do not improve the soil structure and have no nutritional value. However, if applied to damp soil, they reduce water evaporation. They also help suppress weed growth.

*Dry mulches* include natural materials such as straw, leafmould, dry leaves or bracken, as well as horticultural fleece. They are placed in a thick layer over the crown of a plant that is not fully hardy, or tucked around it, as protection from inclement weather in winter.

soil. If the top of the soil is wet but the underneath is still bone dry, carry on until the water has penetrated the first 15–30cm/6–12in of soil.

Some people like to use sprinklers that are left on for a good half hour, soaking different areas of the garden sequentially. My preference is for a leaking hose, which is threaded over the flowerbeds and seeps water gently at low pressure at soil level: the water gets straight to the plants' roots and is not wasted in evaporation. All the leafy growth hides the pipe so it is not unsightly.

Trees and shrubs need regular watering in their first two or three years. After that they will take care of themselves.

## Weeding

Some gardeners like weeding and find it therapeutic while others loathe the task. Like it or not, it simply has to be done. Weeds rob our garden plants of light, water and nutrients and it is best to keep up with them or they can soon take over a perfectly respectable border.

Pull out annual weeds before they have time to flower and set seed. (If you are short of time for a full weeding session, nip off the flower buds to stop them pinging their seed all over the place, triggering a small army of weedlings later on.)

Dig up perennial weeds such as nettles, roots and all; small pieces of root left in the soil will grow into new plants.

Weedkillers may leave residues in the soil and they are difficult to apply precisely. If you feel the need to use a weedkiller, choose a glyphosate-based product, which is applied to plant foliage and is inert once it hits the soil, allowing other plants to grow in the same spot. However, it has no way of discerning between a desirable plant and a weed, so be careful when applying it.

You are better off having regular weeding sessions, as mistakes can prove expensive. If you are not sure what is a weed and what is not, let it grow a bit and you will soon see if it's something undesirable.

## Cutting back

During the growing season, trim any plant foliage that starts to look a little ragged, and deadhead any tall perennials that have finished flowering by cutting off the whole stem at the bottom, just above the basal leaves.

Most herbaceous perennials (apart from evergreens) die down naturally after the growing season, with the onset of autumn or winter. The majority can be cut back lightly when they've finished flowering, and plants that have masses of flower, such as lavender and rosemary, grow leggy if you don't trim off all the faded flowers.

Personally, I cut back any straggly-looking perennials in late autumn, to keep the beds looking tidy and prevent the decaying foliage harbouring pests or diseases – but I leave any plants that offer appealing skeletal

### DEADHEADING

Deadheading is easy and enjoyable. Simply break off any spent flowers by pinching them between your thumb and fingers, or snip them off with a pair of scissors or secateurs.

Removing dead flowers keeps the garden tidy and, more importantly, induces some plants, such as roses, to put out a second flush of flowers later in the same year. It may also extend the flowering season: once they have flowered, most plants start making seed, so cutting off the faded flowers can fool the plant into producing yet more flowers instead.

If a plant is a prolific self-seeder, removing the flowering stems prevents it seeding too freely, but leave the flowers if you want to collect the seed or the seed heads are attractive.

winter shapes to ghost the flowerbeds as long as possible.

In early spring, cut any remaining plant material back to ground level (i.e. as near to the ground as the foliage allows, which will be a little above soil level). Remove all the brown rotting foliage and whatever stems are left, pulling them away by hand or using secateurs. Some perennials put out new shoots early in spring. Be careful to remove the dead material without injuring the new growth hidden among it: don't cut them back too severely, and leave their crowns above ground level. If the plants have formed a large clump, work your way through it in sections. For a smaller clump, one swift scissoring of the secateurs may be all that's needed.

## Pruning

Pruning small trees and shrubs is surprisingly easy. A great many of the trees and shrubs in this book need minimal pruning: the most you need do is cut out any weak, spindly, dead or damaged growth and shorten extra long shoots that are growing out of line and spoiling the shape. Some, particularly evergreens, prefer not to be pruned at all. Deciduous shrubs and climbers may need some pruning to help them keep their shape, grow strongly and put out better flower displays. (For guidance on pruning roses, see pages 36–7.)

You will need a clean, sharp pair of secateurs for cutting slender growth on shrubs and trees, and a strong pair of loppers or a pruning saw for cutting through thicker branches. Make angled cuts, about 6mm/¼in above an outward-facing bud, so that the next branch or stem grows away from the centre of the shrub.

Specific instructions are given in the relevant profiles, but as a general rule of thumb, prune deciduous trees when they are

### PRUNING WISTERIA

Wisterias are pruned twice a year, once in late summer and again in late winter. This ensures they make some flowers, rather than a large amount of leafy growth.

After flowering, in July or August, new shoots will grow at a great rate in all directions. Leave any whippy, long shoots until February pruning. Tie in any strong new stems you want to keep to fill gaps in the framework and cut the rest back to 30cm/12in from the main lateral stem. Fresh growth will appear from these shortened stubs: this is what you are encouraging to flower next year.

In February, cut away any dead, diseased or damaged wood. Then cut back the summer-pruned side shoots to two or three buds from the old, darker coloured woodier growth. In the coming weeks the fat, stubbier buds that produce the flowers will begin to develop (the thinner green buds produce new shoots). Remove all the unwanted whippy shoots, and cut back the stems that have been tied in to fill gaps to five or six buds.

dormant, in late autumn or winter, and prune early-flowering shrubs and climbers once flowering is over. (If you can see flower buds, don't cut them off or you'll have no flowers.) Some plants make flowers on this year's growth: trim these back in early spring, before new growth begins.

Always start with the three Ds, cutting out dead, diseased or damaged wood. After removing old stems and branches you will be able to see what needs to be done more clearly. Now remove any spindly stems, congested growth in the centre of the plant or wayward stems growing out of line at the sides and spoiling the shape. Over time, shrubs may grow leggy, with all the flowers at the top and bare stems at the bottom. Cut back a third of the stems to ground level each year, to encourage new vigorous growth.

Some trees and shrubs grow to such a size and height that pruning becomes impossible. Don't worry; if the plant is thriving but is too big to prune, leave well alone.

# Hardiness

The hardiness rating of a plant provides a reliable indication of the minimum temperatures it needs to survive. Low temperatures can prevent some plants developing well; flower buds may fail to open, and leaves may fall prematurely. If the temperature falls below the plant's level of tolerance for any length of time, it will need some form of protection to prevent lasting damage or fatality.

### Fully hardy: hardy to -15°C/5°F

This term describes perennials, climbers, shrubs, trees and other plants that are naturally tough enough to withstand a lowest winter temperature of -15°C/5°F without suffering lasting harm. They don't need any extra mollycoddling. Plants that fall into this category originate in cold climates and are naturally adept at coping with cold, winds and frosts.

### Frost hardy: hardy to -5°C/23°F

Plants in this category can withstand temperatures as low as -5°C/23°F. Once temperatures dip below this, especially if they stay low for any length of time, the plant may suffer lasting harm or even death. To protect their roots from being frozen and their top-growth from being terminally damaged by frosts they need to be protected with horticultural fleece or provided with shelter, such as a frost-free porch, polytunnel, conservatory or greenhouse.

Pack fleece around the base of a plant, to protect the roots, or wrap it around the plant itself and tie with garden twine, to provide protection for the leaves and stems. Mulch the crowns of vulnerable plants with dry leaves, fern fronds or straw, and wrap containers in bubblewrap or old sacking. The idea is to provide a winter layer, rather like a scarf, to absorb the worst of the weather so it can't affect the plant directly.

### Borderline

Plants are sometimes on the borderline between two classifications, such as fully hardy and frost hardy, and may be adversely affected by cold snaps. Even plants that have been labelled fully hardy can be affected by prolonged periods of bitterly cold weather in cold regions or exposed sites. If in doubt, provide cover.

As our climate changes, we can consider growing plants outside that were previously thought too tender to survive. City dwellers and people gardening in mild areas in the south and west have little trouble growing frost hardy species without any winter protection. I have found they will even survive a severe winter if the roots are well mulched in late autumn and they are sited

Allspice (*Calycanthus floridus*), a fully hardy plant that has scented bark, flowers and roots

There are a variety of ways to protect susceptible plants and seedlings from the effects of cold and frost

against a warm, sheltered wall from the outset. In colder areas, it is still possible to grow frost hardy species if you can provide them with frost-free shelter such as a porch or greenhouse.

Sometimes you may have to dash around the garden, scraping snow from susceptible plants (cordylines loathe snow in their crevices) or providing fleece for plants that are looking feeble. Eventually, experience will lead you to make the right decisions for your garden plants and you'll know when to take a risk – or not as the case may be. And you can always take a cutting earlier in the year or divide the plant in spring as an insurance policy in case of a fatality.

### Half hardy: hardy to 0°C/32°F
Plants in this category will withstand temperature drops down to 0°C/32°F. Give them frost-free shelter or protect their roots

and top-growth with horticultural fleece and dry mulches. Cloches and cold frames also offer useful protection from ice, wind, snow and excessive wet, providing a microclimate for the plants and seeds sheltering under them. In spring, when the weather warms up, they act as a mini-greenhouse, allowing plants to come on faster than those planted in open ground. Be aware that the use of these has to be carefully judged: they have no frost thermostat as in a greenhouse and tender plants can be damaged.

### Frost tender: not hardy below 5°C/41°F
Frost-tender plants will not survive severe winters without protection, and are often grown as annuals in this country. Overwinter in fleece, under cloches or in cold frames, or keep in a warm greenhouse or conservatory and move outside in the summer months, once all risks of frost have gone. Many of these plants will need a period of hardening off before they can be moved back outside from their protected environment (see page 118).

# Problems

Every garden falls prey to pests or diseases at one time or another, but by and large plants are cheerful charges, and they respond enthusiastically to light, air and water.

Pests usually leave obvious signs of their presence, such as leaves with ragged holes or unsightly, notched edges. Slugs, snails, caterpillars are the most common culprits and are easily visible: all you have to do is physically remove them. The more stealthy pests, such as capsid bugs, work at high speed and hide as soon as your shadow falls across the plants.

Plant diseases and infections can be troublesome but are rarely fatal. Although it is harder to recognise that a plant is suffering from a disease than to spot an attack by pests, most are easily treated and many can be avoided altogether by practising good garden hygiene and plant husbandry. Keep an eye out for anything unusual, such as nibbled leaves or wilting foliage, and take appropriate action. Treat your plants well and let them do the rest.

The scarlet lily beetle (left)
Potentially deadly honey fungus (right)

## TIPS FOR DISEASE-FREE PLANTS

- Wash pots and seed trays before use.
- Buy healthy plants.
- Grow disease-resistant varieties.
- Choose the right plant for the growing conditions.
- Avoid planting too closely together, to increase air circulation.
- Feed and water plants regularly.
- Mulch plant roots to prevent them drying out.
- Clear up fallen leaves where fungal spores can overwinter.

# LEAF AND STEM PESTS

**Aphids** are a group of pests, including blackfly, greenfly, whitefly and lupin aphid (or greyfly), about 3mm/⅛in long, with transparent bodies in various colours. They always occur in large numbers, and suck the sap from young shoots of almost any plant, excreting sticky honeydew. The leaves and stems curl and distort, and new growth is damaged.

Spray as often as needed with a few drops of washing-up liquid mixed with water. Encourage beneficial wildlife (the natural enemies of garden pests) into the garden by putting up nesting boxes or making a shallow pond. Alternatively, use a proprietary insecticide.

**Cabbage root fly** larvae feed on the roots of any of the brassica family; transplanted plants are the most vulnerable. Leaves develop a blue tinge and wilt for no apparent reason; young plants can die.

Place plastic or cardboard collars round the base of young plants.

**Capsid bugs** are pale green sap-sucking bugs, some 6mm/¼in long, which damage leaf tips and pepper leaves with tiny holes. Flowers may also be damaged or distorted. They hide on the undersides of leaves, so are difficult to spot.

Check plants regularly and use a proprietary insecticide.

**Caterpillars** eat unsightly holes in plant leaves and are usually easily visible (silky webbing on leaves is also an indicator of their presence).

Pick off by hand; for a large infestation on relatively few leaves, remove the leaves and destroy them. Chemical controls are available.

**Earwigs** are familiar brown insects, just under 2cm/¾in long, with a set of pincers at the rear. They nibble leaves and flowers and tend to feed at night, so it is difficult to stop them unless you are prepared for midnight vigils.

The damage is unsightly, but new leaf growth will disguise it. To make earwig traps, stuff plastic pots with straw and place them upside down on canes among the plants. Alternatively, use a proprietary insecticide.

**Eelworms** are microscopic nematodes that inhabit the stems and leaves of herbaceous perennials (particularly chrysanthemums and phlox). Symptoms include stunted, distorted stems and yellowing leaves.

Dig up and burn or otherwise dispose of affected plants. For new plants, free of eelworms, take root cuttings. There are no chemical or biological controls available.

**Flea beetles** are small, shiny blue-black beetles, about 3mm/⅛in long, that attack the upper surface of a leaf (mainly stocks and wallflowers), causing small, round, shallow holes. Heavy infestations can stunt the growth of mature plants and kill seedlings.

Clear up fallen leaves and rotting stems in autumn, to prevent the beetles hibernating through the winter. Chemical sprays are available.

**Gall midges** are small white or orange maggots, about 2mm/1/16 in long, that feed on plant leaves. Symptoms include leaves that roll up, hiding their silky cocoons. Leaves may thicken abnormally, and plant growth is stunted.

Remove all affected parts of the plant, including shoots. There is no chemical control available.

**Gall mites** are tiny sap-sucking bugs that cause shoot and flower bud distortion, resulting in flowers failing to develop.

Remove all affected parts of the plant, including shoots. There is no chemical control available.

**Leafhoppers** are green or yellow sap-sucking insects, about 3mm/⅛in long, that hop from plant to plant when foliage is disturbed. They cause yellowy discolouration and leaf mottling, but the damage is not serious.

Prop yellow sticky flypaper in the leaves, or spray with a proprietary insecticide.

**Leaf miners** are the larvae of beetles, moths and flies. They mine through plant leaves, leaving telltale brown and white tunnel patterns on the surface.

Pick off affected leaves and dispose of them (if you have a bonfire, burn them). Alternatively, use a proprietary insecticide.

**Lupin aphid** see **Aphids**

**Mealybugs** are tiny pinkish grey sapsuckers, about 6mm/¼in long, which look very much like tiny woodlice and are clothed in an impermeable waxy layer, making them hard to eradicate. They affect anything grown in a pot in a greenhouse or conservatory, and tender young leaves on outdoor plants.

Mix water with a few drops of washing-up liquid and spray the affected plant (the fatty acid in the liquid will dissolve the protective wax coating); use this organic method as often as needed. Alternatively, spray with a proprietary insecticide.

**Narcissus bulb fly** is a small, bee-like, hovering orange-brown fly, some 8mm/⅛in long, which lays its eggs at the base of daffodils and some other bulbs. The young larvae burrow into the bulbs, leaving them hollow. Plants fail to flower or rot away.

Dig up affected bulbs and dispose of them; plant new bulbs elsewhere. Always buy fresh, firm, disease-free bulbs and avoid planting bulbs that have a spongy or hollow feel. Rake up soil around the withering foliage to deter the fly from laying eggs.

**Narcissus eelworms** are microscopic nematodes, invisible to the naked eye, which inhabit the bulbs of daffodils and other bulbs. Early symptoms are yellowed leaf growth, and bulbs eventually rot. If you suspect your plants are affected, cut through a bulb and look for concentric brown ringing.

Dig up and burn or otherwise dispose of affected plants. Eelworms can spread through the soil to neighbouring plants, so do not replant the area with bulbs susceptible to eelworms for two years. Always buy healthy bulbs from a reputable source. There are no chemical or biological controls available.

**Red spider mite** is a sap-sucking mite which affects pot-grown greenhouse or conservatory plants and is hardly visible to the naked eye. It causes leaves to mottle or suddenly turn yellow and makes silky webs around the leaves and stems of plants.

Spray the underside of leaves with an upturned hose from the start of the growing period, to prevent colonisation, and keep greenhouse humidity levels high by hosing down inside daily. Biological controls such as *Phytoseilus persimilis* are successful if introduced early in the season. Red spider mite is very resistant to chemical sprays.

**Sawfly larvae** are small, white to green caterpillars with downward-pointing brown heads, about 1.5cm/⅝in long, which graze on plant leaves in spring, eventually reducing them to a skeleton of veins.

Pick off caterpillars by hand. Alternatively, use a recommended chemical spray.

**Scale insects** The tiny brown, yellow, black, white or grey shells or scales of these sap-sucking insects are found on plant stems or, more commonly, the undersides of plant leaves. Infestation may lead to very poor growth, and secondary infections such as **sooty mould** may set in.

A small attack is unimportant, but a heavy infestation can be very damaging to a plant. Apply methylated spirits to the leaves, with cotton wool or a cotton bud, or use a proprietary organic or chemical spray.

**Scarlet lily beetle** is a bright red beetle, about 6mm/ ¼in long, that lays its eggs on the undersides of lily leaves. The grubs and adult beetles eat holes in the leaves, so that the following year's bulbs may be undersized and fail to flower.

Spray leaves early with olive oil or neem oil to prevent infestations. Pick off bugs by hand and remove any leaves with eggs underneath. Alternatively, use a proprietary insecticide.

**Slugs and snails** have a legendary appetite for leaves and flowers. Look for slime trails and leaf damage: leaf damage close to the bottom of the plant is more likely to be caused by slugs, and top leaf damage by snails.

Fill a small plastic dish with beer or sugar water and place it in the soil near the plant. Slugs and snails are lured by the sugary liquid and drown. Alternatively, sprinkle a few slug pellets around the plants. Biological controls are available.

**Thrips** (commonly known as thunderflies) are small black sap-sucking insects, up to 2mm/¹⁄₁₆in long, which feed on the leaf surface of many plants, causing silvery patches and black dottings. Flower buds may be distorted or fail to open. An infestation can look like a bout of mildew.

Spray with an organic plant oil spray. Alternatively, use a proprietary insecticide.

**Viburnum beetle** larvae are creamy white and about 8mm/⅜in long. They eat viburnum leaves in early summer, reducing them to a tracery of veins. The adult beetles graze on the leaves in late summer, laying their eggs on young shoot tips.

The damage is unsightly, but rarely serious. Remove and dispose of all affected leaves, thereby getting rid of the eggs too. Encourage birds to feed on the larvae by placing bird feeders near by.

**Vine weevil** commonly affect plants grown in containers, but can also damage plants in open ground. The adult beetle (about 1cm/½in long) has a long, pointed snout, and feeds on the leaves of herbaceous plants and shrubs, making notches along their edges. This is unattractive, but rarely fatal. The real damage is done by their larvae, which feed on plant roots. Plants grow poorly and die, often with little warning.

A nematode is available (a form of parasitic microscopic eelworm that enters the larvae and releases bacteria that kill the grubs). To add to their effectiveness, the nematodes keep reproducing inside the dead grub. Alternatively, water pots with a chemical drench.

## PHYSICAL BARRIERS

Many animals leave obvious damage behind them and you will need to create barriers to stop their foraging.

Deer and rabbits can both be a major problem if your garden backs on to unfenced countryside. They eat green shoots and buds, and tear bark from trees. Animal-proof fencing and rabbit guards round young tree trunks are the best defence against these invaders.

Mice and squirrels are professional nibblers of bulbs. Pegging chicken wire over an area that is full of bulbs may help, but it is difficult to keep a determined scavenger away.

Snails have a voracious appetite for leaves and flowers

# PLANT DISEASES

**Blackspot** is a fungal disease affecting roses and is commonly seen during prolonged wet weather, as it is spread by water splashes and rain. Black markings appear on the leaves, which drop off prematurely.

Remove and dispose of all infected foliage. Spray plants with skimmed milk mixed with water at weekly intervals. Alternatively, use a proprietary spray. Plant resistant varieties.

**Blossom wilt** is a fungal infection that affects fruit trees. The flowers and leaves brown and wither, looking scorched, but they remain on the tree; spurs and branches die back if left untreated.

There is little to be done once a tree is infected. Limit damage by pruning out affected twigs and removing diseased or damaged fruit and fallen plant debris.

*Botrytis* **(grey mould)** is a very common fungal disease that affects weak plants of all kinds and flourishes in poor air circulation or damp conditions. Grey, fluffy mould containing spores is clearly evident on the plant and, if handled carelessly, will disperse in the air.

It is spread through the air, which makes it difficult to control, but good growing conditions and plant hygiene do much to prevent it. Remove all affected parts of the plant, cutting back to healthy growth. Burn infected material or dispose of in a bin, but do not add to the compost heap.

**Bud blast** is a fungal disease that affects rhododendrons. The unopened flower buds blacken and are covered with slight hairy growth.

Remove and burn all affected flower buds as the spores can live on for three years, even when the bud is dead, and will continue to spread.

**Canker** Bacterial or fungal cankers affect fruit trees, causing shallow depressions on the bark, usually near a pruning wound or near buds. Growth can die back and fruit may rot.

Prune out dead spurs and shoots in summer and burn all diseased material. Spray with Bordeaux mixture in late summer and early autumn. Grow disease-resistant varieties.

**Clematis wilt** usually occurs on a clematis that is about to flower. The leaves turn grey and part of the plant dries to a crisp or the whole plant may collapse unexpectedly. If not caught early, clematis wilt is potentially fatal.

Remove and destroy infected growth as it appears and give the plant a generous feed and thorough soaking. Plant clematis deeply, with a few buds below soil level, so that new healthy buds are available if the plant dies.

**Clubroot** is a soil-borne infection that affects members of the brassica family and is almost impossible to control, as spores remain in the ground for years and are spread on boots and tools. Symptoms include wilting leaves and yellowing, stunted growth. Plant roots may be distended or swollen.

Dig up and burn all affected plants, and do not plant susceptible plants in the same spot. When growing plants from seed, use fresh, sterilised compost and well-scrubbed pots. A clubroot drench or dip is available.

**Coral spot** is a fungal disease that affects trees and shrubs, causing bright orange pustules on the bark. By the time the disease is noticed, the woody stems are already dead. It usually only attacks an ailing plant, and can be triggered by drought.

Prune out affected shoots and stems to healthy tissue and burn or dispose of infected material but do not compost. Disinfect tools after use.

**Downy mildew** is a fungal disease affecting annuals and perennials. Leaves develop brown and yellow blotches, and have a fuzzy white growth underneath. If left untreated, the plant may die.

Remove any affected leaves immediately, water at the base of plants rather than overhead, thin leaves to improve air circulation and avoid planting too closely together.

**Fireblight** is a bacterial infection that is potentially very serious if not treated early. The flowers blacken and wither; once advanced, leaves yellow, then blacken; ultimately, weeping cankers appear on woody stems or branches.

Prune out infected branches and stems immediately, cutting back to healthy growth. Burn all the material and disinfect the pruning saw to avoid infecting other plants. If the plant is too far gone, dig it up and burn it.

**Gladiolus corm rot** Corms become dry and blackened, often with dark brown raised ridges at the base.

Only use corms that are clean, plump and healthy. Destroy any that are soft or discoloured.

**Honey fungus** is a potentially fatal disease affecting the roots of trees, shrubs and climbers. The fungus also lives on dead or decaying plant matter. The plant grows poorly and honey-coloured toadstools may appear at its base. There may be black bootlace-like threads or white fungal growth with a distinct smell of mushrooms under the bark at the base of the plant; in advanced cases this will also be in the soil.

There are no known remedies. Dig up and remove the affected plant immediately, including as much root as possible, to prevent the spread of the disease. Remove and destroy rotting tree stumps and decaying leaves that can harbour the fungus. Keep plants healthy with a good watering and mulching regime to reduce their susceptibility. Replant the area with plants that are less vulnerable to the disease.

**Ink spot** is a fungal disease that affects bulbous plants. Symptoms include black rotting patches on the bulbs themselves or inky blotches on the leaves.

Spray with Bordeaux mixture and/or dig up and destroy all infected plants. Don't replant bulbs in the area as the disease can stay in the soil.

**Leaf spot** is caused by bacteria or fungi and affects many plants, including perennials. Brown patches with a halo of yellow appear on the leaves and gradually spread. They may be unsightly, but do not cause serious harm.

Remove affected leaves immediately and burn or dispose of in a bin. Thin leaves to improve air circulation and avoid planting too closely together. Water the plant at the base, rather than overhead.

**Lilac blight** is a bacterial infection which occurs after excessive wet weather. Symptoms include blackened buds and wilting stems and shoots.

Burn or dispose of all affected stems or branches. Spray with copper sulphate annually, before the buds open.

**Narcissus basal rot** is a serious, soil-borne fungal disease that affects narcissi. Foliage can yellow early and plants may not flower. Bulbs become slightly soft and brown as the rot spreads.

Lift infected bulbs and discard. Lift healthy bulbs immediately after flowering and replant in another spot, free of the disease. Buy disease-resistant bulbs and discard damaged bulbs.

**Peach leaf curl** is a fungal disease that attacks young, emerging leaves, which curl up and are blistered. Mature leaves are no longer vulnerable.

Pick off affected leaves. As a preventive measure, spray the whole tree with Bordeaux mixture in January and again in mid-February.

**Peony wilt** is a fungal disease affecting the base of peony stems. It can strike just before the flower buds open. Shoots and leaves wither and brown and/or stems may be covered in fuzzy grey mould. If left untreated, the plant collapses and dies.

If a whole plant is stricken, dig it up and burn it (don't add to the compost heap). If only some stems are affected, cut them out below soil level. Thin leaves to increase air circulation; don't overwater or overfeed. No chemical controls are available to the domestic gardener.

**Powdery mildew** is a common fungal disease that affects many plants and is easily recognisable as a white powder on the leaves, which grow stunted or distorted. It is caused by poor air circulation and poor growing conditions.

Remove all affected parts of the plant. Water plants regularly. Improve air circulation by thinning leaves. Proprietary fungicidal sprays are available, but prevention is better than cure.

**Root rots** are soil-borne fungal diseases that affect the roots of trees, shrubs and woody plants when soil is wet or waterlogged. Symptoms include areas of browning leaf that die back. Scrape the stem: blackish discolouration of the exposed tissue is a sure sign of infection.

Keep an open, well-drained soil. Preventive sprays are available for healthy plants, but once a plant is badly affected the only solution is to dig it up and burn or otherwise destroy it.

**Rose ball** occurs in wet weather, when rose buds and blooms become mushy, then brown on the stem, without ever opening.

Removed spoiled flowers and wait for new buds to grow.

**Rose soil sickness** generally occurs when an old rose is dug up and a new rose planted in the same position. Fungal bacteria that remain in the soil attack the new rose, which never grows well and may even die.

Either remove all the soil and replace with fresh compost when planting a new rose, or plant it in another area where roses have not been previously grown: bacteria can remain in the soil for years.

**Rust** is a fungal disease found in moist, damp conditions. Round patches of orangey brown pustules develop on the undersides of leaves. If left unchecked, the life of the plant is at risk.

Good hygiene is the surest way to limit rust. Remove infected leaves from the plant and pick up all fallen leaves; burn infected material if possible. Prune plants to improve air circulation.

**Silver leaf** is a fungal infection that affects trees and shrubs. Leaves develop a silvery lustre and there may be brown stains on stems or branches. Spores are spread by rainfall, splashing and dirty pruning tools. Branches die if left untreated.

Cut infected wood back to 15cm/6in beyond the staining, to healthy white tissue, and seal with wound paint; destroy all the pruned material. Prune in summer when trees are less vulnerable to attack. Grow disease-resistant varieties when possible.

**Sooty mould** is a fungus that grows on honeydew excreted by aphids and other sapsuckers. It is unsightly but relatively harmless. If too much of the leaf surface is covered, it cuts out light, impairing the health of the plant.

Wash leaves down with washing-up liquid and hose them clean. This will also remove aphids and mealybugs and so prevent honeydew forming (alternatively, use a proprietary insecticide).

**Stem rots** are fungal and bacterial diseases, spread by water, that attack plants at their roots, causing them to grow poorly, blacken and rot; the stems and leaves become stunted and discoloured, and can also rot and die.

Dig up and dispose of rotten plants. Don't weed or hoe too close to the base of the plant, as this can damage the stems and lead to infection. Improve drainage and plant at the same depth as the pot.

**Verticillium wilt** is caused by a soil-borne fungus. The plant's roots die and it collapses unexpectedly. If a plant wilts for no obvious reason, cut through the stems, which may reveal telltale brown striping.

Dig up affected plants and burn them. Don't plant similar plants in the same place for several years. There are no chemical controls available to the domestic gardener.

**White blister** is a fungal disease that affects members of the brassica family. White blistering appears on leaves, stems and flowers, and plant growth may be swollen or distorted. It is an airborne complaint, spread by rain, insects and water splashes.

Remove affected parts of the plants and burn them; do not add to a compost heap as spores remain in plant debris and soil for months. There are no chemical controls available.

# Propagation

Many plants, including trees, shrubs and perennials, are easily grown from seed. But there are certain plants for which other methods, such as taking cuttings, division or layering, are more successful: some take a long time to reach a worthwhile size when grown from seed, are notoriously difficult to germinate or don't come true from seed.

## Growing plants from seed

Some seeds germinate very easily. Others are more particular about the amount of warmth and light they need to germinate successfully. Growing plants from seed usually starts in autumn or spring: follow the guidelines in the profiles and on seed packets about when to sow specific plants.

### Sowing seed

Seeds that need a little encouragement to germinate are initially grown indoors, in pots or seed trays on a windowsill or in a greenhouse. To get started, you will need:

- clean pots or seed trays
- fresh potting compost
- watering can with a rose head
- plant labels and pencil

Fill the pots or seed tray with fresh compost, to about 2.5cm/1in below the top of a pot, or 1cm/½in below the top edge of a seed tray, and press the surface down firmly. Water the soil lightly, using a watering can with a rose attachment on the spout so the compost doesn't form uneven troughs. If you are using a greenhouse, give the compost a light drenching of Cheshunt compound before sowing to prevent 'damping off' (which causes seedlings to wither overnight).

Sprinkle small seeds evenly but thinly over the compost surface. If the seeds are large, place one on the top of the soil in a pot. Dust a thin layer of compost over the seeds; using a soil sieve will ensure even coverage. Water the pot or tray carefully, so you don't wash the seeds out. Label each pot or tray.

If sowing indoors, put the seeds on a warm windowsill or leave in a frost-free greenhouse. Some seeds need the extra warmth of a heated greenhouse. As an alternative, a heated propagator is an economical and reliable investment that ensures seeds get the right amount of warmth. Follow any

---

## COLLECTING SEED

Collecting seed from plants in the garden is a good way to raise new plants from old favourites, and it's free. (However, seed taken from hybrid plants ($F_1$) won't necessarily come true, so for these plants the shape, colour and flowers may not be the same as the plant from which the seed was collected.)

Always collect ripe seed from healthy plants. Seed heads are ready for seed collection when they are brown, dry and brittle; ripe seed is normally hard, yellow, black or brown in colour, and separates easily from the seed pod. Unripe seed pods are usually green and still fleshy; the seeds inside may be soft, and are often green or white; they may be sticky or difficult to separate from the pod.

Harvest the ripe seed before the seed pod opens and scatters it. Break off the mature seed cases and crack them open or rub them between your fingers to release the seed inside over a piece of newspaper. Separate the chaff from the seed.

Store the seeds in small, brown paper envelopes (not plastic bags as this will make them rot). Label and date each envelope. Store the sealed envelopes in an airtight container until ready for sowing, normally in spring. Most seeds can be saved and stored, but germination is usually more reliable if ripe seed is sown immediately after collection.

Pricking out passionflower seedlings

are in a greenhouse or on a windowsill, keep them at the specified temperatures and avoid any sudden changes. Seedlings are very fragile at this stage and need careful handling.

As the seedlings grow they will become overcrowded. They need 'pricking out', or transferring into separate pots, allowing them room to develop. Choose the strongest seedlings and gently ease each one out of the compost with a pencil or dibber. Handle them by the leaves, not the stem: they can grow new leaves, but they cannot grow a new stem if it is damaged in handling. Firm each seedling into its new pot gently with your finger or the end of a pencil. Make sure there are no air pockets around the base of the transplanted seedling and water regularly. If you have sown one seed per pot, you can skip this stage and just keep watering your plant as it grows bigger.

instructions about minimum temperatures and keep temperatures constant during germination and growth.

Sow ripe seed in pots, as described above, then place the pots in a cold frame. Close the lid of the frame in winter, to keep them warm, or provide extra insulation with horticultural fleece, straw, sacking or bubblewrap.

## Caring for seedlings

The first sign that the seeds have germinated will be the emergence of tiny green pinheads attached to thin white stems on the surface of the compost. Once the seedlings appear, water them regularly, keeping the compost moist but not waterlogged.

If the seedlings are in a heated propagator, start opening the vents to regulate the air temperature as they grow; if the pots or trays

## Hardening off

Plants that have been grown in protected, indoor conditions need a period of 'hardening off' to acclimatise them to the cold before being planted outside: once all danger of frosts has passed, young plants are gradually exposed to outdoor air temperatures over a period of several weeks.

In a greenhouse, open the vents for a couple of hours a day to start with, to allow colder air to circulate. For plantlets grown in pots in a cold frame, open the lid for a few hours, or if you are growing on a windowsill, leave the window open. Over two or three weeks, slowly increase the number of hours the plants are exposed to daytime temperatures. They should then be sufficiently tough to brave it outdoors. If your plants flag when planted in the ground, you may have hurried them along too fast: protect them with fleece at night and start the daytime exposure again.

# Growing plants from cuttings

Some perennials and shrubs are propagated from cuttings. This method is used for plants that can't be successfully divided or easily grown from seed. A cutting is a small portion of an existing plant that is detached from the plant using a sharp knife, and then grown on in a separate pot to produce a new plant. Choose cutting material from a healthy, vigorous plant and take the cuttings in the morning, when plants are turgid and full of water.

**Softwood cuttings** are taken from a young side shoot, cut just below a leaf joint or node (they are sometimes referred to as **nodal cuttings**). They are normally taken in spring and early summer, when there is new growth on the plant, and they have a good success rate. However, they need to be handled carefully and are prone to wilting, so speed is of the essence.

Choose a healthy non-flowering side stem, about 10cm/4in long with three to four pairs of leaves on it, and cut it away cleanly from the original plant. With a sharp knife, make a clean cut just below a node or leaf joint and strip away all the bottom leaves, leaving just the top two leaves and a bare stem. The final cutting should be about 5cm/2in long.

Holding the cutting gently by the leaves, dip the cut end lightly into hormone rooting powder, tapping off any excess. This is optional, but can speed up rooting. Make a hole in a prepared pot filled with potting compost and insert the upright cutting, firming it down gently. Water, using a fine spray, and label. To help retain moisture and warmth, put a clear plastic bag over the pot and hold it in place with an elastic band, or use a heated propagator.

Once the cuttings have rooted (this will take a number of weeks), either plant out in

Grow American witch hazel (*Fothergilla major*) from softwood cuttings taken in summer

the garden or pot up separately, growing them on until they are large enough to plant out in their final positions.

**Basal stem cuttings** Taken from the strong new shoots that emerge at the base of the plant in spring, these can be quicker to root than traditional softwood cuttings.

Detach a short stem with new leaves, about 5–8cm/2–3in long, from as close to the root as possible. With a sharp knife, trim the bottom of the cutting below a node, removing all the leaves on the lower part of the stem and leaving two or three leaves at the top. Pot up as described above.

**Greenwood cuttings** These are taken from the soft tips of a plant when the stems are still young and pliable, but not too fragile, and beginning to firm up (normally early to mid-summer). They are not as delicate in handling as softwood cuttings, and less prone to wilt. They are taken earlier in the year than semi-ripe cuttings.

Identify a young side shoot or stem that is firm but bendy. Detach it at the point where it joins the older growth. The cutting should have a single main stem and several leaf shoots coming off it. Trim off the soft top shoots just above the node, to leave a cutting about 25cm/10in long with three leaf nodes. With a sharp knife, trim any remaining large leaves to half their size, to reduce moisture loss. The cutting should now look like a single stem with two winged leaves at the top. Nick the base of the stem with a sharp knife and pot up as before, inserting the cutting deep enough to stand upright.

**Semi-ripe cuttings** These are usually taken later in the growing season than greenwood cuttings, from mid-summer to autumn, and are best for woody-based plants and nearly all shrubs, or for plants that don't come true from seed, such as lavender. Semi-ripe cuttings are easier to handle and less liable to wilt than softwood cuttings, but they often take longer to root. Cuttings are taken from this year's growth that is just beginning to harden.

Choose a non-flowering shoot that is soft and green at the tip and slightly firmer at the base and take a cutting about 10–15cm/4–6in long. Make a straight cut below a leaf joint (node) and remove all leaves from the lower stem of the cutting, leaving two or three leaves at the top. The final cutting should be about 5cm/2in long and have two or three pairs of leaves. Pot up as usual.

**Hardwood cuttings** are taken from autumn to spring, when plants are dormant. They are an easy, reliable way to propagate deciduous trees and shrubs.

Choose a healthy mature stem about 30cm/12in long from near the base of the shrub, ensuring it has at least three buds on it. Cut the stem from the plant, using a sharp garden knife or secateurs. Hold the cutting with the buds facing upwards and make a clean, sloping cut just above the top bud and a flat straight across cut below the bottom bud. The cutting should be about 15cm/6in long, with a bud (with the sloping cut above it) at the top, a middle bud and bottom bud.

Repeat this process with additional stems. Either tie a small batch together with a piece of twine and insert the blunt ends into a pot filled with a mixture of sand, gravel and compost, or pot up cuttings individually. Alternatively, scrape a slit trench with a trowel, about 5cm/2in deep, and push single or multiple cuttings down into the earth, making sure they are not touching. Bury them to about half their length and firm the soil back around them. Label the cuttings clearly and leave them in peace until the following autumn, when they will have rooted.

**Root cuttings** Taken from the vigorous young roots of a plant, root cuttings are normally used to propagate plants that produce suckers or shoots from the root area. They are taken when the plant is dormant, usually from late autumn to winter.

Lift a plant and cut off a healthy young root, about as thick as a pencil. Replant the original plant. Using a sharp knife, cut the root into pieces about 4cm/1½in long, making a straight cut at the top end and an angled cut at the bottom. Wash off the soil, pat the cuttings dry with a paper towel and dust them with a fungicide. Insert the angled end of each cutting into a prepared pot of compost, leaving the flat end just visible above the surface. Cover with a thin layer of sharp sand, water and label, and place in a cold frame or greenhouse. The cuttings should be rooted by the following spring.

## Simple layering

Layering is a method of making new plants from climbing plants and many shrubs that are difficult to propagate from cuttings. It is practically idiot proof.

For climbers, layering is normally carried out from late winter to spring. Choose a healthy trailing stem and weight it with a stone or pin it to the ground with a metal peg. Alternatively, fill a pot with compost, bury it so the top is level with the soil surface and peg the trailing stem over the top of the pot; cover it lightly with compost and water well. In either case, the pegged section of stem will produce new roots a few months later. Snip the original stem either side of the rooted section, lift and pot up (or lift up with the buried pot) for a new rooted plant.

Layer evergreen shrubs in spring and deciduous shrubs in autumn. Choose a flexible shoot from the outside of the shrub and anchor it at a leaf node about 30cm/12in down from the top of the stem. Continue as above, severing the rooted section from the parent plant after about twelve months.

**Rooted runners** Some plants reproduce through natural layering. They send out stems (or runners) across the surface of the soil, and these develop new roots at the nodes. Cut the rooted stem into sections, each one with leaves and roots attached, and pot up until the plants are large enough to grow on outdoors.

## Dividing perennials

Division is one of the easiest and most reliable ways to multiply plants. They are simply divided into two or more parts and replanted. This method is often used for plants that have a clump-forming or carpeting habit, but most perennials can be propagated by division.

It is normally carried out before flowering in spring, when the plant is just beginning to

### DIVIDING RHIZOMES

Rhizomes are thick, fleshy underground stems from which roots grow. Over time, they can become congested in plants such as iris, which reduces their flowering.

The ideal time to divide a rhizomatous plant is when it is dormant. Dig it up carefully, trying to avoid damage to the rhizomes, and shake off the soil so you can see what you are doing. Pull the clump apart and separate out the healthy, non-woody rhizomes that have active growth on them (discard the old rhizomes). Trim any broken roots with a sharp knife and then cut the leaves in half, to reduce water loss from the new plantlets.

Either pot them up individually or replant them about 25cm/10in apart in full sun or partial shade, with the tip of the rhizome just visible above the soil.

Dividing a hemerocallis rootball – an easy way to multiply plants

the process to make smaller clumps, all with good visible root systems. If the roots are very fibrous and tough, use a sharp knife to cut the sections into manageable segments. If the original clump is small, either use a knife or gently tease the roots apart by hand.

It is best to replant sections taken from the outer edges of a clump, discarding the older, tougher segments from the centre. Plant the new clumps straight into their final planting positions, if they are large enough, or grow them on in pots of compost until they are ready to transplant.

Puzzlingly, the profiles in this book may tell you that a plant resents disturbance and then suggest that you propagate it by division. This means that the plant won't like being dug up and divided. However, needs must, so divide it as gently as possible, without bruising the roots too much, and give the newly planted clumps a good watering and a mulch of organic matter. The new plants may sulk for a growing season but they soon buck up.

grow and there are few leaves: this reduces water loss and rooting will occur more quickly. It can also be done in autumn, when the soil is still warm, encouraging plants to develop new roots before the onset of winter. When dividing plants in autumn, cut back the leafy growth by at least half, to reduce the burden on the roots.

To divide a large clump, dig up the plant, roots and all, and prise the rootball apart using two forks back to back. Or, brutal though it may seem, slice through the root system with a sharp spade. Repeat

## PROPAGATING BULBS

Many bulbs multiply underground quite naturally, although tulips will reduce in number with age. It can take several years to grow a fair-sized bulb from seed, so it is easier to plant up the baby bulbs or 'offsets' and grow them on.

Dig up a clump of overcrowded bulbs once the foliage has died down and separate the offsets from the adult bulbs (they come away quite easily). Clean them of loose soil, dust with fungicide and pot up individually. Leave them in the pot for several seasons to bulk up before planting out into the garden.

Treat corms in a similar way. Gently pull off the new cormlets attached to the mature corms, pot them up in fresh compost and overwinter before planting out in spring. It will be two or three years before they flower.

# The gardening year

## Spring

In February or March, remove dead stems from the American witch hazel (*Fothergilla major*) before it flowers. Prune shrub, patio and bushy roses in April and cut back buddlejas. Prune *Drimys winteri* after flowering.

This is a perfect time for planting. If you sowed sweet peas (*Lathyrus odoratus*) last October, plant them out into final positions in April or transplant early spring-sown plantlets in May; don't let them dry out.

Get on top of seasonal tasks, so you are not overwhelmed later. Spread about 10cm/ 4in of well-rotted organic matter or mushroom compost over the flower and shrub beds. Keep up with the weeding, and don't forget to stake any plants that need support.

## Summer

Trim the faded flower heads of rhododendrons where practical, to help them bloom more profusely next year. Deadhead roses and sweet peas to prolong their flowering and keep the borders looking tidy.

Tie in the new growth of climbing roses, and make earwig traps for clematis, roses and chrysanthemums (see page 111). Plant *Amaryllis belladonna* in a warm, sheltered position outside and take cuttings of lavender and pinks.

## Autumn

Sow sweet peas for an early start next year and plant shrubs while the soil is still warm. Lily of the valley (*Convallaria majalis*) benefits from autumn planting and, if the ground is not frozen, plant some lily bulbs.

Birds are natural allies in combating next year's pests

Renovate your borders and start making plans for next year: cut back straggly perennials, divide large clumps that have outgrown their space and make a note of any short-lived perennials that need replacing.

Make a herb garden in a trough to bring indoors, and pot up some aromatic lemon balm (*Melissa officinalis*) for the kitchen windowsill, for a lift in the dark days ahead.

## Winter

Cut some small stems of sweetly scented sarcococca and bring them indoors as a reminder that life is stirring in the garden. Sow seeds of scented pelargoniums in pots on a warm windowsill or heated porch for bedding and fillers next summer. Winter-prune wisteria.

Make a simple bird table to encourage birds into the garden: they will help you out by eating all your insect plant predators next year. Then get started on building a scented arbour. Roll up your sleeves, and call family or friends to lend a hand. Reward your helpers with home-made soup with crusty bread or tea and home-baked cakes.

# Fragrant plants for specific purposes

Fragrant plants come in all shapes, colours and sizes, which gives you tremendous scope for planning your perfumed garden all through the year. The following categories are intended to help you choose the right plants for your garden space and olfactory tastes.

## Full shade
Camellia sasanqua
   'Crimson King'
Clethra alnifolia 'Paniculata'
Convallaria majalis
Geranium macrorrhizum
   'Bevan's Variety'
Hosta 'Honeybells'
Maianthemum racemosum
   (formerly Smilacena
   racemosa)
Patrinia triloba var. palmata
Polygonatum odoratum
Primula vulgaris
Sarcococca confusa
Skimmia japonica 'Fragrans'
Trillium luteum

## Woodland
Agrimonia eupatoria
Anemone sylvestris
Aquilegia fragrans
Arbutus unedo
Cardiocrinum giganteum
Clethra alnifolia 'Paniculata'
Convallaria majalis
Corylopsis sinensis
Dictamnus albus var.
   purpureus
Dipelta floribunda
Disporopsis pernyi
Edgeworthia chrysantha
Fothergilla major
Galium odoratum
Hamamelis virginiana
Hesperis matronalis var.
   albiflora
Hyacinthus orientalis
   'City of Haarlem'
Impatiens tinctoria
Jasminum humile
   'Revolutum'
Lindera benzoin
Linnaea borealis subsp.
   americana
Lunaria rediviva
Mahonia × media 'Charity'

Maianthemum racemosum
   (formerly Smilacena
   racemosa)
Patrinia triloba var. palmata
Pittosporum tenuifolium
Polygonatum odoratum
Primula vulgaris
Rhododendron fortunei
   'Sir Charles Butler'
R. 'Mary Poppins'
Sambucus nigra 'Gerda'
Schisandra rubriflora
Skimmia japonica 'Fragrans'
Trillium luteum
Viburnum farreri
Viola cornuta Alba Group
V. odorata

## Coastal areas
Anemone sylvestris
Arbutus unedo
Berberis julianae
Cestrum parqui
Cordyline australis
Crambe cordifolia
Cytisus battandieri
Elaeagnus × ebbingei
   'Gilt Edge'
Eriobotrya japonica
Erysimum 'Moonlight'
Escallonia 'Iveyi'
Genista aetnensis
Heptacodium miconioides
Laburnum alpinum 'Pendulum'
Lonicera fragrantissima
L. japonica 'Halliana'
Lupinus 'Noble Maiden'
   (Band of Nobles Series)
Olearia macrodonta
Perovskia 'Blue Spire'
Philadelphus 'Belle Etoile'
Pittosporum tenuifolium
Sambucus nigra 'Gerda'
Spartium junceum

## Drought tolerant
Abelia × grandiflora

Abeliophyllum distichum
Agastache 'Black Adder'
Allium schoenoprasum
A. tuberosum
Aloysia citrodora
Amaryllis belladonna
Arabis alpina subsp. caucasica
   'Flore Pleno'
Arbutus unedo
Artemisia abrotanum
A. absinthium 'Lambrook
   Mist'
A. 'Powis Castle'
Berberis julianae
Buddleja davidii 'Royal Red'
Carpenteria californica
Caryopteris × clandonensis
   'Arthur Simmonds'
Chaenomeles × superba
   'Pink Lady'
Chamaemelum nobilis
   'Flore Pleno'
Chimonanthus praecox
Choisya × dewitteana
   'Aztec Pearl'
Cistus × argenteus
   'Peggy Sammons'
Cordyline australis
Coronilla valentina subsp.
   glauca 'Citrina'
Crambe cordifolia
Crinum × powellii
Cytisus battandieri
Dianthus 'Mrs Sinkins'
Dictamnus albus var.
   purpureus
Dipelta floribunda
Echinacea 'Sunset'
   (Big Sky Series)
Edgeworthia chrysantha
Elaeagnus × ebbingei
   'Gilt Edge'
Eriobotrya japonica
Erysimum 'Moonlight'
Foeniculum vulgare
Galium odoratum
Genista aetnensis

Geranium macrorrhizum
   'Bevan's Variety'
Hamamelis mollis
   'Coombe Wood'
Helichrysum italicum
Hemerocallis dumortieri
Heptacodium miconioides
Hermodactylus tuberosus
Hesperis matronalis var.
   albiflora
Humulus lupulus 'Aureus'
Laurus nobilis
Lavandula angustifolia 'Alba'
L.a. 'Hidcote'
L. stoechas
L. stoechas subsp. stoechas
   f. rosea 'Kew Red'
Leptospermum lanigerum
Lonicera fragrantissima
L. japonica 'Halliana'
L. × purpusii 'Winter Beauty'
Magnolia grandiflora
Mahonia × media 'Charity'
Nepeta 'Six Hills Giant'
Oenothera caespitosa
Olearia macrodonta
Origanum vulgare
Osmanthus × burkwoodii
Passiflora caerulea
Pelargonium 'Attar of Roses'
Perovskia 'Blue Spire'
Phuopsis stylosa 'Purpurea'
Pittosporum tenuifolium
Ribes odoratum
Rosa 'Bobbie James'
R. Ginger Syllabub
R. 'Guinée'
R. 'Ispahan'
R. Kent
R. Regensberg
R. 'Maigold'
R. rubiginosa
R. xanthina 'Canary Bird'
Rosmarinus officinalis
Santolina pinnata subsp.
   neapolitana
Sarcococca confusa

Scabiosa atropurpurea
Skimmia japonica 'Fragrans'
Spartium junceum
Syringa vulgaris
  'Madame Lemoine'
Thymus pulegioides
  'Bertram Anderson'
T. serpyllum 'Pink Chintz'
Verbena rigida
Viburnum farreri
Wisteria sinensis

### Ground cover
Camellia sasanqua
  'Crimson King'
Caryopteris × clandonensis
  'Arthur Simmonds'
Cistus × argenteus
  'Peggy Sammons'
Coronilla valentina subsp.
  glauca 'Citrina'
Dianthus 'Mrs Sinkins'
Disporopsis pernyi
Elaeagnus × ebbingei
  'Gilt Edge'
Galium odoratum
Heliotropium arborescens
  'Chatsworth'
Linnaea borealis subsp.
  americana
Mahonia × media 'Charity'
Maianthemum racemosum
  (formerly Smilacena
  racemosa)
Olearia macrodonta
Patrinia triloba var. palmata
Phuopsis stylosa 'Purpurea'
Skimmia japonica 'Fragrans'
Viola cornuta Alba Group
V. odorata

### Hedging
Abelia × grandiflora
Berberis julianae
Buddleja davidii 'Royal Red'
Elaeagnus × ebbingei
  'Gilt Edge'
Escallonia 'Iveyi'
Lavandula angustifolia
  'Hidcote'
Lindera benzoin
Mahonia × media 'Charity'
Olearia macrodonta
Osmanthus × burkwoodii
Philadelphus 'Belle Etoile'
Pittosporum tenuifolium
Rhododendron
  'Mary Poppins'

Ribes odoratum
Rosa Regensberg
R. xanthina 'Canary Bird'
Sarcococca confusa
Viburnum × bodnantense
  'Dawn'
V. farreri

### Slopes and banks
Camellia sasanqua
  'Crimson King'
Caryopteris × clandonensis
  'Arthur Simmonds'
Choisya × dewitteana
  'Aztec Pearl'
Cistus × argenteus
  'Peggy Sammons'
Coronilla valentina subsp.
  glauca 'Citrina'
Corylopsis sinensis
Elaeagnus × ebbingei
  'Gilt Edge'
Galium odoratum
Linnaea borealis subsp.
  americana
Mahonia × media 'Charity'
Olearia macrodonta
Patrinia triloba var. palmata
Phuopsis stylosa 'Purpurea'

### Containers
Alstroemeria 'Sweet Laura'
× Amarcrinum memoria-corsii
Amaryllis belladonna
Anemone sylvestris
Aquilegia fragrans
Arabis alpina subsp.
  caucasica 'Flore Pleno'
Brugmansia × candida
  'Grand Marnier'
Calycanthus floridus
Camellia sasanqua
  'Crimson King'
Carpenteria californica
Chimonanthus praecox
Chlidanthus fragrans
Chrysanthemum
  'Carmine Blush'
Clematis 'Jan Fopma'
Clerodendrum trichotomum
Cordyline australis
Coronilla valentina subsp.
  glauca 'Citrina'
Crinum × powellii
Daphne cneorum 'Eximia'
Dianthus 'Mrs Sinkins'
Dregea sinensis
Drimys winteri

Edgeworthia chrysantha
Erysimum 'Moonlight'
Galanthus 'S. Arnott'
Gardenia jasminoides
  'Kleim's Hardy'
Heliotropium arborescens
  'Chatsworth'
Hemerocallis dumortieri
Hermodactylus tuberosus
Hosta 'Honeybells'
Hyacinthus orientalis
  'City of Haarlem'
Illicium anisatum
Impatiens tinctoria
Iris 'Harmony' (Reticulata)
Itea ilicifolia
Lamatia myricoides
Lathyrus odoratus 'America'
Lonicera fragrantissima
Loropetalum chinense
  f. rubrum 'Fire Dance'
Matthiola incana
Narcissus 'Tripartite'
Oenothera caespitosa
Olearia macrodonta
Oxalis enneaphylla
Paeonia 'Eden's Perfume'
Phuopsis stylosa 'Purpurea'
Pittosporum tenuifolium
Primula vulgaris
Prunus mume 'Beni-chidori'
Rosa 'Guinée'
R. 'Ispahan'
R. Kent
R. Regensberg
Sarcococca confusa
Scilla mischtschenkoana
  'Tubergeniana'
Trachelospermum jasminoides
Verbena rigida
Viola cornuta Alba Group
V. odorata
Vitaliana primuliflora

### Architectural
Angelica archangelica
Brugmansia × candida
  'Grand Marnier'
Camellia sasanqua
  'Crimson King'
Cordyline australis
Eriobotrya japonica
Foeniculum vulgare
Hedychium forrestii
Itea ilicifolia
Magnolia 'Susan'
Mahonia × media
  'Charity'

### Climbers and wall shrubs
Abeliophyllum distichum
Akebia quinata
Azara serrata
Carpenteria californica
Cestrum parqui
Chaenomeles × superba
  'Pink Lady'
Chimonanthus praecox
Clematis armandii
C. rehderiana
Dregea sinensis
Humulus lupulus 'Aureus'
Itea ilicifolia
Jasminum humile 'Revolutum'
Lathyrus odoratus 'America'
Lonicera fragrantissima
L. japonica 'Halliana'
Loropetalum chinense
  f. rubrum 'Fire Dance'
Magnolia grandiflora
Passiflora caerulea
Ribes odoratum
Rosa 'Bobbie James'
R. Ginger Syllabub
R. 'Maigold'
R. xanthina 'Canary Bird'
Schisandra rubriflora
Stauntonia hexaphylla
Trachelospermum jasminoides
Wisteria sinensis

### Evergreen
Abelia × grandiflora
× Amarcrinum memoria-corsii
Arabis alpina subsp.
  caucasica 'Flore Pleno'
Arbutus unedo
Artemisia absinthium
  'Lambrook Mist'
Azara serrata
Camellia sasanqua
  'Crimson King'
Carpenteria californica
Choisya × dewitteana
  'Aztec Pearl'
Cistus × argenteus
  'Peggy Sammons'
Coronilla valentina subsp.
  glauca 'Citrina'
Daphne cneorum 'Eximia'
Dianthus 'Mrs Sinkins'
Disporopsis pernyi
Dregea sinensis
Drimys winteri
Elaeagnus × ebbingei
  'Gilt Edge'

Erysimum 'Moonlight'
Escallonia 'Iveyi'
Geranium macrorrhizum
    'Bevan's Variety'
Helichrysum italicum
Illicium anisatum
Itea ilicifolia
Jasminum humile
    'Revolutum'
Lamatia myricoides
Laurus nobilis
Lavandula angustifolia 'Alba'
L.a. 'Hidcote'
L. stoechas
L. stoechas subsp. stoechas
    f. rosea 'Kew Red'
Leptospermum lanigerum
Linnaea borealis subsp.
    americana
Lonicera japonica 'Halliana'
Loropetalum chinense
    f. rubrum 'Fire Dance'
Magnolia grandiflora
Mahonia × media 'Charity'
Olearia macrodonta
Osmanthus × burkwoodii
Passiflora caerulea
Pelargonium 'Attar of Roses'
Pittosporum tenuifolium
Prostanthera cuneata
Rhododendron fortunei
    'Sir Charles Butler'
Rosmarinus officinalis
Santolina pinnata subsp.
    neapolitana
Sarcococca confusa
Skimmia japonica 'Fragrans'
Stauntonia hexaphylla
Thymus pulegioides
    'Bertram Anderson'
T. serpyllum 'Pink Chintz'
Trachelospermum jasminoides
Viola cornuta Alba Group
V. odorata
Vitaliana primuliflora
Wisteria sinensis

**Foliage**
Artemisia abrotanum
A. absinthium
    'Lambrook Mist'
A. 'Powis Castle'
Caryopteris × clandonensis
    'Arthur Simmonds'
Chamaemelum nobilis
    'Flore Pleno'
Eriobotrya japonica
Hedychium forrestii

Helichrysum italicum
Hosta 'Honeybells'
Humulus lupulus 'Aureus'
Leptospermum lanigerum
Loropetalum chinense
    f. rubrum 'Fire Dance'
Myrrhis odorata
Oxalis enneaphylla
Phlox paniculata
    'White Admiral'
Sambucus nigra 'Gerda'
Santolina pinnata subsp.
    neapolitana
Thymus pulegioides
    'Bertram Anderson'
T. serpyllum 'Pink Chintz'

**Autumn leaf colour**
Abeliophyllum distichum
Clethra alnifolia 'Paniculata'
Hamamelis mollis
    'Coombe Wood'
Heptacodium miconioides
Loropetalum chinense
    f. rubrum 'Fire Dance'
Fothergilla major
Lindera benzoin
Rhododendron
    'Mary Poppins'
Viburnum farreri

**Berries, decorative
seed pods/heads, fruits**
Akebia quinata
Anemone sylvestris
Arbutus unedo
Azara serrata
Berberis julianae
Chaenomeles × superba
    'Pink Lady'
Clerodendrum trichotomum
Clethra alnifolia 'Paniculata'
Coronilla valentina subsp.
    glauca 'Citrina'
Daphne cneorum 'Eximia'
Disporopsis pernyi
Dregea sinensis
Elaeagnus × ebbingei
    'Gilt Edge'
Eriobotrya japonica
Foeniculum vulgare
Heptacodium miconioides
Humulus lupulus 'Aureus'
Lathyrus odoratus 'America'
Laurus nobilis
Leptospermum lanigerum
Lindera benzoin
Lonicera fragrantissima

L. japonica 'Halliana'
Lunaria rediviva
Mahonia × media 'Charity'
Maianthemum racemosum
    (formerly Smilacena
    racemosa)
Myrrhis odorata
Olearia macrodonta
Passiflora caerulea
Pittosporum tenuifolium
Polygonatum odoratum
Ribes odoratum
Rosa Kent
R. rubiginosa
Sambucus nigra 'Gerda'
Sarcococca confusa
Schisandra rubriflora
Stauntonia hexaphylla
Viburnum farreri
Wisteria sinensis

**Cream/white flowers**
Abelia × grandiflora
Abeliophyllum distichum
Allium tuberosum
Aloysia citrodora
Anemone sylvestris
Aquilegia fragrans
Arabis alpina subsp.
    caucasica 'Flore Pleno'
Arbutus unedo
Cardiocrinum giganteum
Carpenteria californica
Chamaemelum nobilis
    'Flore Pleno'
Choisya × dewitteana
    'Aztec Pearl'
Clematis armandii
Clerodendrum trichotomum
Clethra alnifolia 'Paniculata'
Convallaria majalis
Cordyline australis
Crambe cordifolia
Dianthus 'Mrs Sinkins'
Disporopsis pernyi
Drimys winteri
Elaeagnus × ebbingei
    'Gilt Edge'
Eriobotrya japonica
Escallonia 'Iveyi'
Fothergilla major
Galanthus 'S. Arnott'
Galium odoratum
Gardenia jasminoides
    'Kleim's Hardy'
Gladiolus murielae
Hedychium forrestii
Heptacodium miconioides

Hesperis matronalis var.
    albiflora
Hosta 'Honeybells'
Illicium anisatum
Impatiens tinctoria
Lamatia myricoides
Lathyrus odoratus 'America'
Lavandula angustifolia 'Alba'
Leptospermum lanigerum
Lilium 'Casa Blanca'
Lonicera fragrantissima
L. × purpusii 'Winter Beauty'
Lupinus 'Noble Maiden'
    (Band of Nobles Series)
Magnolia grandiflora
Maianthemum racemosum
    (formerly Smilacena
    racemosa)
Matthiola incana
Myrrhis odorata
Nicotiana sylvestris
Ocimum basilicum
Oenothera caespitosa
Olearia macrodonta
Osmanthus × burkwoodii
Oxalis enneaphylla
Passiflora caerulea
Philadelphus 'Belle Etoile'
Phlox paniculata
    'White Admiral'
Polygonatum odoratum
Prostanthera cuneata
Rhododendron fortunei
    'Sir Charles Butler'
Rosa 'Bobbie James'
R. Kent
Sarcococca confusa
Scilla mischtschenkoana
    'Tubergeniana'
Skimmia japonica 'Fragrans'
Stauntonia hexaphylla
Syringa vulgaris
    'Madame Lemoine'
Trachelospermum jasminoides
Viburnum farreri
Viola cornuta Alba Group

**Yellow/orange flowers**
Agrimonia eupatoria
Alstroemeria 'Sweet Laura'
Artemisia absinthium
    'Lambrook Mist'
A. 'Powis Castle'
Azara serrata
Berberis julianae
Brugmansia × candida
    'Grand Marnier'
Cestrum parqui

# Plant index

## Picture credits

Photographs supplied by Garden World Images Ltd.

Lindera benzoin (p.23) © Elaine Haug/Smithsonian Institution;
Rhododendron fortunei 'Sir Charles Butler' (p.26) © Millais
Nurseries; × Amarcrinum memoria-corsii (p.39) © Floramedia;
Linnaea borealis subsp. americana (p.46) © Hartside Nursery
Garden; Paeonia 'Eden's Perfume' (p.48) © John Scheepers
Flower Bulbs (www.johnscheepers.com); Clematis 'Jan Fopma'
(p.57) © Clematis on the Web/Ian Lang; Laburnum alpinum
'Pendulum' (p.62) © Floramedia; Rosa Ginger Syllabub (p.65)
© Harkness Roses